ISSUES THAT CONCERN YOU

Zero Tolerance Policies in Schools

Peggy Daniels, *Book Editor*

GREENHAVEN PRESS
A part of Gale, Cengage Learning

GALE
CENGAGE Learning

Detroit • New York • San Francisco • New Haven, Conn • Waterville, Maine • London

Christine Nasso, *Publisher*
Elizabeth Des Chenes, *Managing Editor*

For more information, contact:
Greenhaven Press
27500 Drake Rd.
Farmington Hills, MI 48331-3535
Or you can visit our Internet site at gale.cengage.com

For product information and technology assistance, contact us at

Gale Customer Support, 1-800-877-4253
For permission to use material from this text or product, submit all requests online at www.cengage.com/permissions

Further permissions questions can be emailed to permissionrequest@cengage.com

Articles in Greenhaven Press anthologies are often edited for length to meet page requirements. In addition, original titles of these works are changed to clearly present the main thesis and to explicitly indicate the author's opinion. Every effort is made to ensure that Greenhaven Press accurately reflects the original intent of the authors. Every effort has been made to trace the owners of copyrighted material.

Cover image Sascha Burkard, 2008. Used under license from shutterstock.com

LIBRARY OF CONGRESS CATALOGING-IN-PUBLICATION DATA

Zero tolerance policies in schools / Peggy Daniels, book editor.
    p. cm. — (Issues that concern you)
  Includes bibliographical references and index.
  ISBN 978-0-7377-4189-6 (hardcover)
1. School discipline—United States. 2. Classroom management—United States. I. Daniels, Peggy.
  LB3012.2.Z46 2008
  371.50973—dc22

                                                                2008022300

Printed in the United States of America
1 2 3 4 5 6 7 13 12 11 10 09

CONTENTS

Z ero tolerance policies have been in place at most U.S. public schools for more than a decade. These policies impose strict penalties for certain forbidden behaviors, like bringing a weapon to school, with no exceptions. Many students have been directly affected by such policies, or know someone who has. Once widely praised as the most effective way to ensure safety at school, zero tolerance policies are now being criticized as unfair to students. This controversy raises a number of questions about school safety and student discipline. Where did zero tolerance policies come from? Why did zero tolerance policies become so widely used in schools? Are these policies working, or have they caused more problems than they solve? These points, along with many other aspects of the zero tolerance policy issue, are addressed in this volume.

The Origin of Zero Tolerance Policies in Schools

Zero tolerance policies were implemented in most U.S. schools as a result of the Gun-Free Schools Act (GFSA), which became a national law in October 1994. The GFSA was intended to ensure the removal of firearms from public schools by requiring mandatory punishments for anyone who brings a gun to school. These strict disciplinary policies became commonly known by the name "zero tolerance," although that phrase does not actually appear in the wording of the GFSA law.

The GFSA requires all schools that receive money from the federal government to follow specific rules in order to continue being funded. These rules include:

- The establishment of a policy banning guns from school
- The mandatory expulsion of any student possessing a gun at school
- The mandatory immediate reporting of any student possessing a gun at school to the police
- The mandatory annual reporting of all student expulsions to the U.S. Department of Education

Because the majority of public schools need government funding to stay open, the GFSA effectively blanketed the U.S. public school system with these requirements.

Although the GFSA imposed mandatory expulsion for any student who brings a gun to school, a student who faces punishment under a school's zero tolerance policy is legally entitled to an investigation and hearing. These rights are guaranteed by the U.S. Constitution as well as most state constitutions. Under GFSA requirements, student punishment should be determined by the results of the investigation and hearing. Under certain circumstances—if, for example, a student has brought a weapon other than a gun to school—the GFSA allows the time period of mandatory expulsions to be decided on a case-by-case basis. The GFSA is very clear, however, that any student who is found to be in possession of a gun at school must be expelled for one year.

In 1994, when the GFSA was enacted, it was estimated that 100,000 guns were brought into American schools every day. The first official evaluation of the impact of the GFSA was conducted in 1997 and included statistics from 29 states. This evaluation showed a significant reduction in the number of guns found in schools, indicating that the GFSA was initially successful. During the 1995–1996 school year, school officials expelled approximately 6,000 students for possession of dangerous weapons, with the majority of those cases involving guns.

The Growth of Zero Tolerance Policies in Schools

Although early reports indicated that GFSA requirements could effectively reduce the number of guns in schools, school violence continued to worsen. In 1999, the problem of escalating gun violence in schools became a national concern after the tragic events of April 20 at Columbine High School in Littleton, Colorado, when two students killed fifteen people (including themselves) and wounded twenty-three. This became one of the worst incidents of school violence to date, causing a renewed public outcry over issues of school safety and violence prevention.

Many schools toughened their zero tolerance policies in response, restricting more types of behavior and making punishments more severe. During 1999 and 2000, schools voluntarily expanded their zero tolerance policies beyond the GFSA requirements, banning a wider variety of weapons, potential weapons, and controlled substances such as drugs and medication, and forbidding destructive activities such as stealing and graffiti. Although private schools are not normally bound by the GFSA because they do not usually receive federal funding, many chose to implement GFSA-inspired zero tolerance policies as a way of preventing school violence. Lawmakers and school officials hoped that a more widespread implementation of zero tolerance policies in schools would help to stem the tide of violence and make schools safer.

However, as the use of zero tolerance policies grew in schools, the rules became complicated and confusing. Policies that began with simple efforts to protect students gradually became more restrictive and troublesome. The implementation of punishments and disciplinary actions became more uneven instead of more consistent. As accusations of unfair discipline grew, zero tolerance policies in schools quickly became controversial.

The Backlash Against Zero Tolerance Policies in Schools

By 2002, initial public support for zero tolerance policies in schools had been replaced by public outrage over the long-term effects of unfair discipline on students and their families. Stories of poorly implemented zero tolerance policies made news headlines with increasing frequency. A growing number of students were being expelled for bringing to school items that would not ordinarily be defined as dangerous, including plastic eating utensils, key chains, craft scissors, prescription medication, and certain pieces of jewelry. Students and parents became confused about which items were allowed and which were not. Meanwhile, serious incidents of violence were still occurring in schools across the country.

Zero tolerance policies can dramatically affect the relationship between students and their teachers and administrators.

Parents, educators, and lawmakers were beginning to question the value of overly strict school discipline policies. Public debate focused on the idea that schools may have gone too far with efforts to protect students from violence. In arguing against the use of mandatory expulsions required under harsh zero tolerance policies, the American Bar Association observed that a child is three times more likely to be struck by lightning than to be killed violently at school. The use of zero tolerance policies in schools was re-evaluated, with the goal of determining how to keep schools safe without resorting to overly restrictive policies that were difficult to enforce fairly.

Examining Zero Tolerance Policies in Schools

In *Issues That Concern You: Zero Tolerance Policies in Schools*, authors debate the effectiveness and fairness of such policies in excerpts from articles, books, reports, and other sources. In addition, the volume also includes resources for further investigation. The "Organizations to Contact" section gives students direct access to organizations that are working on issues surrounding zero tolerance policies in schools. The bibliography highlights recent books and periodicals for more in-depth study, while the Appendix "What You Should Know About Zero Tolerance Policies in Schools" outlines basic facts and statistics. Finally, the "What You Should Do About Zero Tolerance Policies in Schools" section helps students use their knowledge to help themselves and others. Taken together, these features make *Issues That Concern You: Zero Tolerance Policies in Schools* a valuable resource for anyone researching this issue.

ONE

Strict Student Discipline Is Necessary to Make Schools Safer

Public Agenda

> Public Agenda is a nonprofit public opinion research organization founded in 1975 by pollster Daniel Yankelovich. The following Public Agenda report provides an overview of student behavior and discipline problems in middle schools and high schools throughout the United States. The authors draw on random sample surveys of more than thirteen hundred teachers and parents. Most respondents agree that strict discipline is needed in the school setting but feel that schools do not always enforce disciplinary policies fairly. The report shows that school discipline is one of the most important challenges that face educators today. The statistics and analysis in the report show many different perceptions of the problem and disagreement over the causes. Teachers and parents also indicate how school administrators can address the school discipline problem more effectively, including strong support for zero tolerance policies.

Too many students are losing critical opportunities for learning—and too many teachers are leaving the profession—because of the behavior of a few persistent troublemakers. What's more, say teachers, today's misbehaving students

Public Agenda, "Teaching Interrupted: Do Discipline Policies in Today's Schools Foster the Common Good?" May 2004. Copyright © 2004 Public Agenda. Reproduced by permission.

are quick to remind them that students have rights and their parents can sue.

These are some key findings in *Teaching Interrupted: Do Discipline Policies in Today's Public Schools Foster the Common Good?* based on national random sample surveys of 725 middle and high school teachers and 600 parents of middle and high school students. The surveys offer a detailed look at the discipline issue, exploring its causes, the effectiveness of current policies, the impact on school climate and receptivity to various solutions. . . .

The School Discipline Problem

According to the study, teachers operate in a culture of challenge and second-guessing—one that has an impact on their ability to teach and maintain order. Nearly half of teachers (49%) complain that they have been accused of unfairly disciplining a student. More than half (55%) say that districts backing down from assertive parents causes discipline problems. Nearly 8 in 10 teachers (78%) say that there are persistent troublemakers in their school who should have been removed from regular classrooms. Both teachers and parents support a variety of remedies, ranging from more special schools for misbehaving students to removing monetary awards for parents who sue.

Discipline has been a recurring theme in public opinion research on public schools for years, and *Teaching Interrupted* suggests that educators have made only limited progress addressing it. The issue continues to bedevil teachers, concern parents and derail learning in schools across the country.

It's almost unanimously accepted among teachers (97%) that a school needs good discipline and behavior in order to flourish, and 78% of parents agree. It's also widely accepted among both groups that part of a school's mission—in addition to teaching the three R's [colloquial expression for reading, writing, and arithmetic]—is to teach kids to follow the rules so they can become productive citizens (93% and 88%).

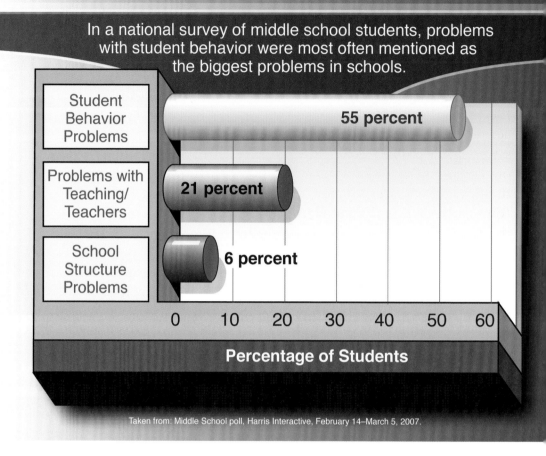

Student Behavior Is the Most Commonly Cited Problem in Middle Schools

In a national survey of middle school students, problems with student behavior were most often mentioned as the biggest problems in schools.

Student Behavior Problems — 55 percent

Problems with Teaching/ Teachers — 21 percent

School Structure Problems — 6 percent

Percentage of Students

0 10 20 30 40 50 60

Taken from: Middle School poll, Harris Interactive, February 14–March 5, 2007.

Current Discipline Policies Are Not Working

Yet, the observations of both teachers and parents collected in this study suggest that today's school discipline policies may not be working in the interest of the common good. For example:

The vast majority of both teachers (85%) and parents (73%) say the school experience of most students suffers at the expense of a few chronic offenders. Most teachers (78%) report that students who are persistent behavior problems and should be removed from school grounds are not removed.

Students pay a heavy price academically when schools tolerate the chronic bad behavior of the few. Most teachers (77%) admit their teaching would be a lot more effective if they didn't have to spend so much time dealing with disruptive students. Similarly, many parents (43%) believe their child would accomplish more in school if teachers weren't distracted by discipline issues.

Lack of parental support and fear of lawsuits are ever-present concerns for many teachers. Nearly 8 in 10 teachers (78%) say students are quick to remind them that they have rights or that their parents can sue. Nearly half (49%) say they have been accused of unfairly disciplining a child. More than half (52%) say behavior problems often stem from teachers who are soft on discipline "because they can't count on parents or schools to support them." Nevertheless, approximately 7 in 10 teachers (69%) and parents (72%) say it's just a handful of parents in their own school who challenge or threaten to sue when their child is disciplined.

Many teachers say documentation requirements go beyond common sense. Although relatively few teachers (14%) reject the need to document incidents of misbehavior as too cumbersome, more than 4 in 10 (44%) say the requirements in their own school "go beyond common sense" and are used primarily to protect the schools from potential lawsuits. The overwhelming majority of teachers (79%) would reserve the use of special hearings—where witnesses are called and lawyers are present—for only the most egregious discipline cases.

Student discipline and behavior problems are pervasive. More than half of the teachers surveyed (52%)—and 43% of the parents—report having an armed police officer stationed on their school grounds, and large numbers indicate that discipline is a concern in their own school. On the whole, the findings suggest that the schools are doing a good job responding to the most serious behavior problems, like drugs and guns, but that they should be doing a lot better when it comes to minor violations of the rules, such as talking out, horseplay, disrespect and the like.

Student discipline takes a toll on teachers. More than 1 in 3 teachers say they have seriously considered quitting the profession—or know a colleague who has left—because student discipline and behavior became so intolerable. And 85% believe new teachers are particularly unprepared for dealing with behavior problems.

Problems with student behavior appear to be more acute in urban schools and in schools with high concentrations of student poverty. Compared with their counterparts, teachers in these schools are more likely to cite student discipline as a top problem, more likely to say it is driving teachers out of the profession and more likely to indicate it has a serious negative impact on student learning.

The Causes of School Discipline Problems

Topping the list of causes of behavior problems in the nation's schools is parents' failure to teach their children discipline (82% of teachers and 74% of parents). Second on the list is: "There's disrespect everywhere in our culture—students absorb it and bring it to school" (73% and 68%). Other Public Agenda research shows that only about a third of parents say they have succeeded in teaching their child to have self-control and discipline, while half say they have succeeded in teaching their child to do their best in school.

Along with inattentive parents and an overall culture of disrespect, teachers and parents also attribute behavior problems to: overcrowded schools and classrooms (62% of teachers and 54% of parents); parents who are too hasty in challenging school decisions on discipline (58% of teachers and 42% of parents); districts that back down from assertive parents (55% of teachers and 48% of parents); and teachers who ease up on discipline because they worry they may not get support (52% of teachers).

Considering Possible Approaches to School Discipline

Despite multiple and complicated causes, the discipline problem is not insurmountable, according to the teachers and parents who participated in this study. In fact, majorities of both teachers and parents voice support for all of the ideas tested in the surveys, although some garner much more intense backing than others.

Effective school discipline policies are more complicated than symbolic signage like this might imply.

The number of respondents who show "very" strong support (as opposed to "somewhat" strong) indicates the intensity of support. The proposals fell into the following categories:

Dealing with "persistent troublemakers." Seventy percent of teachers and 68% of parents strongly support the establishment of "zero-tolerance" policies so students know they will be kicked out of school for serious violations, with another 23% of teachers and 20% of parents indicating they support this idea somewhat (Total support: 93% teachers; 89% parents).

In addition, 46% of teachers and 33% of parents strongly support giving principals a lot more authority to handle discipline issues as they see fit, with another 38% of teachers and 37% of parents supporting this idea somewhat (Total support: 84% teachers; 70% parents).

More than half of teachers (57%) and 43% of parents also especially liked proposals for establishing alternative schools for chronic offenders, with another 30% of teachers and 32% of parents liking this idea somewhat (Total support: 87% teachers; 74% parents).

Putting more responsibility on parents. A strong majority of teachers (69%) say finding ways to hold parents more accountable for kids' behavior would be a very effective solution to the schools' discipline problems, with another 25% saying they think it would be somewhat effective (Total support: 94% teachers).

Limiting lawsuits on discipline. Forty-two percent of teachers and 46% of parents strongly support limiting lawsuits to serious situations like expulsion, with another 40% of teachers and 32% of parents liking this idea somewhat (Total support: 82% teachers; 78% parents).

Fifty percent of teachers and 43% of parents also strongly approve of removing the possibility of monetary awards for parents who sue over discipline issues, with another 32% of teachers and 27% of parents approving somewhat (Total support: 82% teachers; 69% parents).

Consistently enforcing the little rules. Both groups show high levels of support for the "broken windows" approach—strictly enforcing the little rules so the right tone is created and bigger problems are avoided: 61% of teachers and 63% of parents strongly support this, with another 30% of teachers and 25% of parents supporting this idea somewhat (Total support: 91% teachers; 88% parents).

Parents, in particular, think dress codes are a very (59%) or somewhat (25%) good idea (Total support: 75% teachers; 84% parents).

Most teachers believe putting more of an emphasis on classroom management skills in teacher education programs would go a long way toward improving student discipline and behavior: 54% say this would be a very effective solution and another 37% somewhat effective (Total support: 91% teachers).

Teachers also believe that treating special education students just like other students, unless their misbehavior is related to their disability, is a good approach: 65% of teachers say this would be a very effective solution, while another 29% consider it somewhat effective (Total support: 94% teachers).

TWO

Weak Disciplinary Policies Endanger Students and Inhibit Learning

Marc A. Epstein

> Marc A. Epstein is a teacher and academic dean at Jamaica High School in Queens, New York. In the following viewpoint, Epstein argues that despite significant increases in disciplinary and security staff, many schools are out of control. He believes that school discipline problems have worsened each year and that current methods of dealing with disruptive student behavior have not been effective. Epstein also believes that many school administrators have become far too tolerant of students with chronic behavior problems. He argues for the effectiveness of suspensions and expulsions and concludes that students with behavior problems should be removed from schools.

At the height of the baby boom, Jamaica High School in Queens, New York, enrolled approximately 5,000 students, who attended school in triple session. Each cohort of students had to start and end school at a different time in order to maximize classroom use. There were only two or three deans to address disciplinary issues, and a lone patrolman stood watch in the lobby of the school. It was assumed that a large portion of the school's graduates would go on to college, while the rest would become society's secretaries, plumbers, carpenters, printers, and butchers.

Marc A. Epstein, "Security Detail: An Inside Look at School Discipline," *Education Next*, Summer 2003. Copyright © 2008 by the Board of Trustees of Leland Stanford Junior University. Reproduced by permission.

Although Jamaica High was considered one of the school system's academic gems, it also provided vocational training that has long since disappeared.

Today the school population has been sliced to 2,500, yet Jamaica High now has eight deans (myself included), who devote much of their time to disciplinary issues; an assistant principal for security; two secretaries, one part time, one full time; and a school aide assigned just to the dean's office. In addition, ten school security agents employed by the New York City Police Department patrol Jamaica's halls. The number increases on those days when "random scanning" of students for weapons is in effect.

Fewer Students, More Severe Problems

The extra personnel alone do not even begin to account for the costs of attempting to maintain discipline and safety in the school. Consider the following tales from Jamaica High. In one instance, a teacher saw a student take a gun from his locker and show it to other students. He informed the security agent, who in dereliction of his duty did nothing. Then the teacher came to the Dean's Office, and I immediately began looking for the student. But the student had fled the building. When he returned two hours later, the police searched him and found nothing. The superintendent was informed, and an investigation of the event proceeded. The student claimed that he had no gun. When asked why he had exited the building, he claimed that a security agent had thrown him out. He could not identify the agent by sex or by race.

Statements were taken from students who had seen the gun, the student's parents were notified, and a hearing date was set. For the teacher and me to attend the hearing, substitutes had to be hired to cover our classes. At the hearing, after waiting for two hours, we received word that the parent had asked for a postponement by making a telephone call, which was within his rights. It was the end of the school year, so the case was carried over to the next fall. The postponed hearing was scheduled for September 13, which wound up being just two days after the horrible events of September 11. As I walked to the offices located near Madison Avenue and 22nd Street in downtown Manhattan, an acrid stench hung in the air, even though I was some distance from Ground Zero.

At the hearing, the parent of the accused asked me a very good question: Why had we allowed his son back to school if we believed that he had a gun? His son had rights, I said. And it took a couple thousand dollars' worth of personnel hours to protect them. The hearing officer eventually found in our favor, and the student was transferred to another school.

Learning Disabled or Deeply Troubled?

In another instance, a learning-disabled student in a mainstream class asked a teacher for a hall pass. When the teacher refused to give it to him, the student called the teacher, who had badly injured her hand in a car accident, a "crippled bitch" and threw an object at her. A security agent who had witnessed the event removed the student. The superintendent was informed, and the student's home was contacted. The next day I confiscated the hand of a store mannequin that the student was carrying around with him. He said he wanted to show the teacher that "he had a hand like hers." At 16 years of age, the student had earned just one of the 40 credits needed to graduate.

The teacher, the security agent, and I had to appear at the hearing. Again, substitutes were provided to cover our absences. And again, the hearing was postponed, this time at the request of a man who called himself the student's "grandfather." Even though he turned out not to be the grandfather, the hearing officer accepted him as the advocate because he brought a letter to that effect signed by the mother, with whom I was never able to speak.

At the next hearing, the "grandfather" asked the teacher, "Do you consider yourself crippled, because if you do, then you are in fact a 'crippled bitch,' and the charges should be dropped." The hearing officer did not agree and found in the school's favor. However, the student fell under the protections of the federal special-education law because of his diagnosed learning disability. As such, he was allowed to return to the school premises immediately. After several more suspensions, school authorities were finally able to get him transferred to one of the school system's "second opportunity schools," or "SOS" for short.

Multiply this case by thousands, and you will have some notion of the problem of maintaining safety in the city's schools. State and federal court decisions intended to protect the rights of stu-

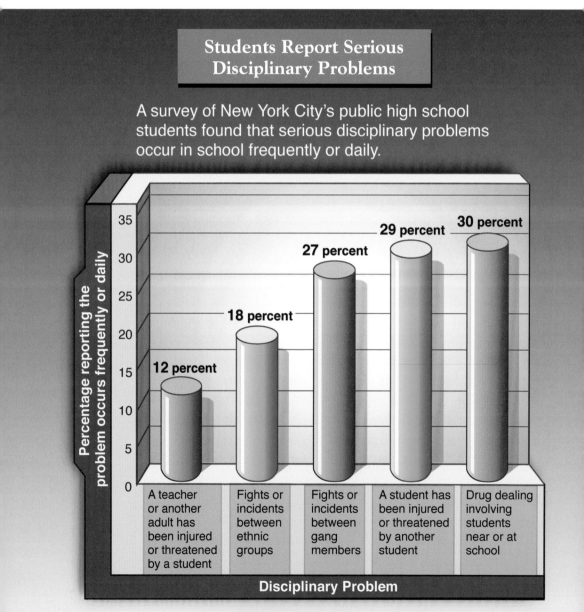

Students Report Serious Disciplinary Problems

A survey of New York City's public high school students found that serious disciplinary problems occur in school frequently or daily.

Percentage reporting the problem occurs frequently or daily

- 12 percent — A teacher or another adult has been injured or threatened by a student
- 18 percent — Fights or incidents between ethnic groups
- 27 percent — Fights or incidents between gang members
- 29 percent — A student has been injured or threatened by another student
- 30 percent — Drug dealing involving students near or at school

Disciplinary Problem

Taken from: Citizens' Committee for Children of New York, 2001/
Education Next, Hoover Institution, Summer 2003.

dents, followed by the schools' attempts to comply with the mindless bureaucratic directives used to implement these rulings, have made it all but impossible to expel a student unless a flagrant felony is committed that results in the student's incarceration. As a result, our halls are filled with students who cut nearly all their classes on a daily basis, whose only contribution to the educational process is to harass other students and make it necessary to maintain a phalanx of security officers at the school.

Strict Discipline Helps Students

At a large high school like Jamaica, the demands of the school day make it nearly impossible to give these deeply troubled kids the kind of individual attention and support they need. They slip through the cracks and wind up disrupting not only their own education, but also that of the students around them. The schools need to be made safe for education, and those who bring chaos to the school environment need alternative education settings, where teachers and counselors can work with them and their families on a more one-to-one basis. This is especially true of students who have committed criminal acts in or outside of school. The New York City Department of Education took a step in the right direction in February 2003, when officials announced plans to open 17 "New Beginnings" centers for students with the most serious behavior problems. However, these centers will accommodate only a fraction of the students who require placement, and red tape has delayed their opening.

Often these children can be targeted for help merely on the basis of their academic progress, but they rarely are. Our worst discipline problems usually present our biggest educational challenges as well. In almost every instance, an investigation of a serious disciplinary infraction reveals that the student has made little or no academic progress. For students who enter high school unable to read, the game is up unless they are identified and placed in an alternative learning environment outside of the high-school setting. Once inside the large New York City high school, they become lost to everyone except the police and the deans.

The High Cost of School Security

It is impossible to account for the pedagogical costs such students exact on the schools: the classroom disruptions, the harassing of other students, and the frustrated new teachers who leave the profession. And the New York City Department of Education has not even attempted to tally the financial costs. Indeed, nobody knows how much of the city's $12 billion-plus annual budget is dedicated to school safety. But we do know that a significant portion of the funds that are earmarked for instruction and administration is actually used to maintain security.

There are approximately 150 high schools in the New York City school system, and a significant share of them house more than 2,000 students. High schools increasingly make security the sole responsibility of an assistant principal, which is supposed to free the school's principal to focus on instructional leadership. The responsibility for the day-to-day enforcement of each school's disciplinary code falls to the dean's office. School deans, whose number varies from school to school, usually teach only two classes a day. Yet at Jamaica High, the salaries and benefits for the eight deans and three-person support staff assigned to school security are treated as part of the instructional and administrative budget. Another 14 school aides are stationed in the cafeteria, outside bathrooms, locker rooms, and halls, in what can certainly be described as security-related assignments. At least $1 million in salary and benefits is devoted to school safety at Jamaica High alone—and that does not include the cost of the ten school safety officers, who are paid through a separate contract with the Police Department.

Problem Students Should Be Removed from School

The situation is routinely aggravated by administrative decisions that fail to recognize the realities of everyday school life. For instance, schools can administer one of two kinds of suspensions, the "principal's suspension" and the more serious "superintendent's suspension." However, the principal's suspension was ren-

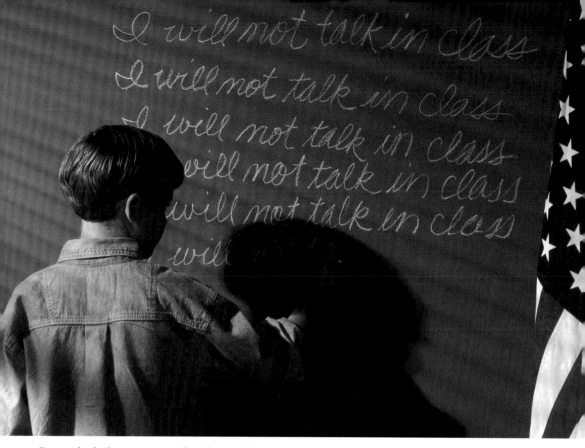

Some feel that many schools need to toughen up their behavior policies.

dered essentially useless when the previous school's chancellor, Harold Levy, ordered that the suspension be served "in house." This was abetted by new state regulations requiring that suspended students not have their education interrupted.

Before Levy changed the rules, the principal's suspension was an effective tool because it kept an unruly student out of the building until at least one of the student's parents accompanied the student to a conference with the principal, the dean, and the guidance counselor. Students prone to misbehaving would think twice if their mother or father had to take off from work to get them readmitted. It also gave school administrators the opportunity to discuss the incident, and usually the student's general lack of academic progress, with the parent. The same conference is supposed to take place after an in-house suspension, but with the student already in school, the parent would often refuse to show up. The principal's suspension effectively withered as our first line of defense.

The granting of a superintendent's suspension hearing allows the student charged with an offense to call and cross-examine witnesses, postpone, and of course appeal the decision. The hearing is held in a special facility with a hearing officer, the dean of record, the victim or victims, witnesses, and a technician who transcribes the testimony. Before the New York state commissioner of education forbade it, students who had charges sustained against them in such a hearing would be moved to another school automatically. Under current policy, if the school believes the student represents a serious threat to the school population, it must initiate an involuntary transfer procedure, involving another round of reports and hearings before the student can be removed. This is essentially a game of musical chairs, only with a guarantee that when the music stops everyone is left with a chair. Should the case involve a "special needs" student, a finding must be made that the offense was not related to the disability. If the disability is ruled to have been a contributing factor, the student is returned to school without consequence.

For instance, one student was hearing voices and stalked a teacher, who had an order of protection issued. The student turned out to be schizophrenic and was removed as an EDP (emotionally disturbed person) on four separate occasions over two years. The father refused to have him institutionalized, despite the recommendation of the school psychologist. He was readmitted again and again. He eventually left the school, much as hundreds of students do each year, just disappearing into the ether without our ever knowing where they wound up. The point is that sizable populations in need of close supervision for a host of problems that often have nothing to do with education are simply left adrift in large city high schools. When their behavior becomes truly disruptive, the system responds with a stream of procedures that expends endless man-hours and appropriates uncountable treasure, often without anything to show for the effort.

Stronger Policies Are Needed

In dealing with the more dangerous members of our student population, the system attempts to ensure safety by disrupting their pattern of behavior. Expulsion is no longer an option, so this is accomplished by using the lengthy involuntary transfer procedure to move the disruptive students to other locations. Eventually, however, cliques of students involuntarily transferred to other schools meet up once again. One is reminded of the film *Escape from Alcatraz*, where Clint Eastwood reconnects with his old cellmates from Joliet and plans his escape from "the Rock" along with them. Recently, the mother of a student who was new to the school called to tell me that her child had been robbed of her new leather coat after getting into an after-school fight with a group of students on Jamaica Avenue. The next day I asked the student, "How were you able to find yourself fighting with another group of students on your very first day?" She said that she had linked up with a bunch of fellow involuntary transfers from Franklin K. Lane High School, who began feuding with girls from Jamaica High. Why we would expect such students to perform any better simply by transferring them to yet another large high school is beyond me.

Since students must be given a fresh start, schools receiving transfers are not informed of the reasons why a new student has been placed in their midst. Even worse, the schools are not informed of arrests outside the school, so felons are admitted without our knowledge on a regular basis. Last year, I spent two months trying to track down a student who had committed a school infraction, only to learn that he had been discharged after 20 days of continuous absence. He was on Riker's Island, awaiting sentencing. Later, after being placed on probation for armed robbery, he was readmitted to Jamaica High. Court decisions and school regulations have ensured a safe haven for some truly dangerous criminals in our schools. Should a student be arrested in school, he can come back the very next day and await the results of school disciplinary action for several days afterward.

In a similar vein, the schools are mandated to educate children who have been removed from their homes by the courts and placed in group homes within our zone. Often they are the victims of the most horrific domestic circumstances. Placed in a school of 2,500 students, in the middle of a school term, what are the odds that they will successfully adjust? In November 2002, the director of a group home informed me that three of her charges had robbed another student and asked me if I wanted them arrested. When I asked her why they were placed at Jamaica, she informed me that there were no other options.

At any given time a high school of 2,000 or more students will have 300 to 400 students who have made no academic progress over the course of two years. A percentage will be passive and simply go to class and fail most of their courses. But a sizable portion will cut class regularly and keep school safety and the deans at bay on a full-time basis. With no high-quality alternative settings to send them to and no power to eject them from the premises, the school safety officers find themselves either herding them into classrooms or bonding with the worst offenders in a sort of reverse "Stockholm syndrome." [Stockholm syndrome refers to a situation in which hostages begin to feel sympathetic loyalty to their captors.]

The Loss of Control

The loss of building control did not happen overnight. Decisions made on a case-by-case basis usually made sense, but when compounded with other "plausible" solutions, they incubated like one of those mysterious building molds that render a structure uninhabitable. For example, high schools used to have a homeroom at the start and end of the school day. On entry, students would lock up their coats and be marked present. At the end of the day, they would report to the room again and get their coats. Especially during the winter, this would help to control the building. Students could not simply walk out if they felt like it or flee if they were in trouble. School authorities could readily spot an intruder wearing a coat while everyone else was in shirtsleeves. It was also a good way to eliminate the problems of coats being stolen and endless confrontations over the wearing of hats and gang-related paraphernalia. During the 1990s, however, the city's teacher union, the United Federation of Teachers (UFT), argued that forcing teachers to supervise homeroom was unprofessional. The union was able to get this effective building-control tool abolished through contract negotiations.

Take another example. School aides were put in charge of supervising the cafeteria after the UFT successfully argued that teachers should not have cafeteria duty. Even some of the severest critics of the UFT agreed that it was a waste of teachers' time for them to be policing the cafeteria. However, teachers knew the students, and the students knew that they knew them. The teachers could keep students in line in a way that school aides never could.

In one fell swoop, the cafeteria became student-gang turf. In Park West High School, a separate cafeteria had to be created for freshmen because they were falling prey to upperclassmen. Naturally, the cafeteria has become a fertile breeding ground for conflict and disorderly behavior that bubbles up daily throughout the school. Students had at least a dose of respect for the school deans and teachers who used to manage the cafeteria. School aides, by contrast, are easily intimidated by students. It is a rare school aide who will confront gang-affiliated students without fear of retribution.

Behavior Problems Should Not Be Tolerated

Not only the teachers but also frequently the parents of disruptive students are shocked by the laxity of the school system. My first superintendent's suspension hearing involved a freshman accused of threatening a female teacher who simply asked him to take his seat and stop cursing. He responded by overturning a desk as he walked toward her, stating he was "going to f—— her up." He was charged with threatening and menacing. The charges against him were sustained, and afterward his mother decided to return him to Trinidad, where the young man was from. When she returned to school to retrieve his records, she informed me that in Trinidad, her son would never have dared to threaten a teacher, and if he did. . . . She did not complete the sentence. I would experience this sentiment time end again. Parental disbelief at the level of tolerance for this kind of behavior is palpable. Yet the only response from policymakers and the courts has been the erection of a costly system of adjudicating, tolerating, excusing, and ultimately ignoring deviant behavior.

Those strolling past the library at Jamaica High School can view the plaques honoring the school's alumni who gave their lives for their country during World War II. Pictures of students, faculty, and athletic teams also adorn the walls. The picture-taking stops sometime during the mid-1970s though. It is as if a geological age had been preserved in a stratified layer of sediment. There was a time, it seems, when the school had a culture and a sense of spirit that invited displays of unity and pride. Something quite meaningful appears to have been lost in the decades since.

Statistically, Jamaica High School falls squarely in the middle of the school system. Learning takes place, and good kids get educated by good teachers, but the presence of a permanent class of "students" who cannot function in this setting continually destabilizes the learning environment, tempts marginal students to behave badly, and squanders untold treasure for no good reason.

THREE

Zero Tolerance Policies Are Not Effective

Russell Skiba

Russell Skiba is a professor at Indiana University and director of the Equity Project, a research consortium focusing on school discipline. He is also a past member of the American Psychological Association Task Force on Zero Tolerance. In the following viewpoint, Skiba argues that zero tolerance policies are not effective. He looks at common assumptions about zero tolerance policies in schools and presents facts that contradict or disprove these assumptions. Skiba concludes that zero tolerance policies do not increase student safety or improve the educational environment.

In the face of serious incidents of violence in our schools in the last decade, the prevention of school disruption and violence has become a central and pressing concern. Beyond the prevention of deadly violence, we know that teachers cannot teach and students cannot learn in a school climate characterized by disruption. A . . . national survey of middle and high school teachers and parents found almost universal support for the proposition that schools need good discipline and student behavior in order to flourish; a large majority felt that the school experience of most students suffers at the expense of a few disruptive students. Clearly,

Russell Skiba, "Zero Tolerance: The Assumptions and the Facts," *Education Policy Briefs*, vol. 2, Summer 2004. Reproduced by permission.

schools have the right and responsibility to use all effective means at their disposal to maintain the integrity, productivity, and safety of the learning climate. About this, there can be no dispute.

Great controversy has arisen, however, about *how* to keep schools safe and productive. [Since the early 1990s], many schools and school districts have applied a disciplinary policy that has come to be known as zero tolerance. The philosophy of zero tolerance, adapted from the war on drugs in the late 1980s, encourages a no-nonsense approach to school discipline, increasing both the length and numbers of suspensions and expulsions for a broader range of behavior. By punishing both serious and less serious disruptions more severely, the goal of zero tolerance is to send a message to potential troublemakers that certain behaviors will not be tolerated.

Examining Zero Tolerance Policies in Schools

Zero tolerance discipline relies upon a certain set of assumptions about schools, violence, and the outcomes of discipline. In the period of heightened fear about school-based violence during the 1990s, it was not always easy to dispassionately examine the evidence for different strategies of violence prevention. It seemed imperative to put an end to school shootings immediately, and those strategies promising the shortest route to that goal were often the most appealing.

In the last few years, however, there has been an enormous amount of study concerning the most promising methods for preventing school violence and promoting effective school learning climates. Unfortunately, much of this evidence has not supported the assumptions that guided the acceptance of zero tolerance discipline in the 1990s. The purpose of this briefing paper is to examine that evidence. To what extent are the promises and assumptions of zero tolerance borne out by our rapidly increasing knowledge about school violence prevention? . . .

Below, we list each assumption commonly associated with zero tolerance, briefly review the evidence concerning that assumption, and close with the facts reflecting the match between the assumption and the research-based evidence.

A security supervisor stands guard as students walk through metal detectors at Chicago's William Howard Taft High School. Many schools use metal detectors to enforce their weapons policies.

School Violence Rates

ASSUMPTION: *School violence is nearing an epidemic stage, necessitating forceful, no-nonsense strategies for violence prevention.*

It is true that there was a substantial increase in youth violence in the early 1990s, an increase that leveled off in the latter part of the decade. Advocates of zero tolerance pointed to the presumed increase in violence in schools as a rationale for a newer, tougher approach to school safety.

Over time, however, we have come to understand that violence is not rampant in America's schools, nor does it appear to be increasing. Data consistently support the assertion of the U.S. Department of Education's Annual Report on School Safety that "The vast majority of America's schools are safe places." Serious crimes involving gangs, weapons, or drugs constitute less than 10% of the problems cited by principals in their schools: where crimes against students occur, the majority of incidents appear to be theft or vandalism, rather than physical attacks or threats with a weapon. With a school homicide rate of less than one in a million, the chances of violent death among juveniles are almost 40 times as great out of school as in school. Nor does there appear to be any evidence that violence is becoming more prevalent in schools. While shocking and senseless shootings give the impression of dramatic increases in school-related violence, national surveys consistently find that school violence has stayed essentially stable or even decreased slightly over time. As noted school violence researcher Irwin Hyman concludes from an examination of these data, "Despite public perceptions to the contrary, the current data do not support the claim that there has been a dramatic, overall increase in school-based violence in recent years."

FACT: Violence and disruption are extremely important concerns that must be addressed in our schools, but national reports have consistently found no evidence that violence is out of control in America's schools, nor that school violence is worsening.

Consistent Discipline

ASSUMPTION: Zero tolerance increases the consistency of school discipline and thereby sends an important message to students.

Unless an intervention can be implemented with some degree of consistency, it is unlikely that intervention can have a positive effect. In particular, behavioral psychologists have argued that punishment, applied inconsistently, will be ineffective and probably lead to a host of side-effects, such as counter-aggression.

Federal policy in the Gun-Free Schools Act of 1994 mandating a one-year expulsion for firearms appears to have increased statewide consistency in response to students bringing weapons to school. But zero tolerance has also been extended to a host of other infractions from fighting to drugs and alcohol to threats to disruption, and these other applications of zero tolerance have resulted in a high degree of inconsistency and controversy.

Discipline Policies Are Applied Inconsistently in Schools

This chart shows the number of school staff at one midwestern school who referred students to the school office for discipline. Note that two-thirds of the disciplinary actions come from one-quarter of the staff.

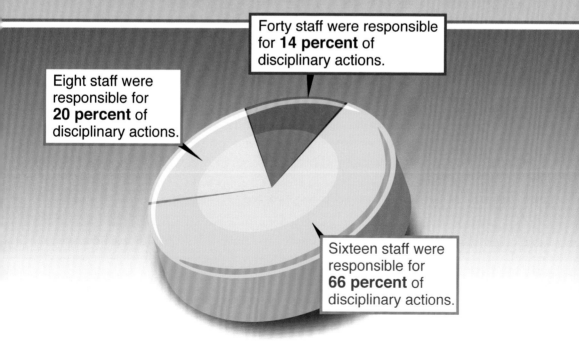

Forty staff were responsible for **14 percent** of disciplinary actions.

Eight staff were responsible for **20 percent** of disciplinary actions.

Sixteen staff were responsible for **66 percent** of disciplinary actions.

Taken from: Russel Skiba, "Zero Tolerance: The Assumptions and the Facts," *Education Policy Briefs*, Indiana Youth Services Association, Summer 2004.

In general, there is wide variation across states, school districts, and schools in how suspension and expulsion are used. Although student behavior does contribute to the probability of discipline, idiosyncratic classroom and school characteristics may be more important than student behavior in determining who will be suspended or expelled. In one study, one-quarter of classroom teachers were found to be responsible for two-thirds of the referrals to the office. School-to-school variability in suspension and expulsion are so great that one set of investigators concluded that students who wish to change their chances of being suspended or expelled "will be better off by transferring to a school with a lower suspension rate than by improving their attitudes or reducing their misbehavior."

FACT: *Beyond federal policy on weapons possession, the consistency of implementation of zero tolerance is so low as to make it unlikely that it could function effectively to improve school climate or school safety.*

School Climate

ASSUMPTION: *The no-nonsense approach of zero tolerance leads to improved school climate.*

Advocates of zero tolerance argue that it makes sense that removing the most troublesome students from a school would lead to an overall improvement in the quality of the learning climate for those students that remain. Once again however, the facts don't support the intuition. Rather than making a contribution to school safety, the increased use of suspension and expulsion seems to be associated with student and teacher perceptions of a less effective and inviting school climate. Schools with higher rates of suspension have been reported to have higher student-teacher ratios and a lower level of academic quality, spend more time on discipline-related matters, pay significantly less attention to issues of school climate, and have less satisfactory school governance. In the long-term, there is a moderate correlation between the use of exclusionary discipline and school dropout. Even more troubling are emerging data suggesting that higher rates of school suspension are associated with lower average test scores on tests of achievement.

FACT: It is difficult to argue that disciplinary exclusion is an essential tool in promoting a productive learning climate when schools that use suspension more frequently appear to have poorer school climates, higher dropout rates, and lower achievement.

Improving Student Behavior

ASSUMPTION: Zero tolerance has made a difference in school safety and improved student behavior.

There are currently no controlled and comprehensive studies that could be used as an evaluation of the effectiveness of zero tolerance at the national level. The most comprehensive data, released by the U.S. Department of Education in its progress report on the Gun-Free Schools Act, showed a change in weapons reports on school campuses over a two-year period after the implementation of the act, but there was also a concurrent change in reporting requirements during that period, making the data all but uninterpretable.

More generally, data on the effectiveness of suspension and expulsion for changing student behavior are not promising. Descriptive studies of school suspension have typically found that 30% to 50% of those suspended are repeat offenders. Such a high rate of recidivism suggests that school suspension is not a particularly effective deterrent to future disruptive behavior. Indeed, in one study, students who were suspended at the sixth-grade level were more likely to be referred to the office or suspended in eighth grade, leading the researchers to conclude that "for some students, suspension functions more as a reinforcer than a punisher."

FACT: Fifteen years after the rise of zero tolerance, and almost ten years since it became national policy for weapons, there is still no credible evidence that zero tolerance suspensions and expulsions are an effective method for changing student behavior.

Student Opinion

ASSUMPTION: Students learn important lessons from the application of zero tolerance, and ultimately feel safer.

The purpose of the application of punishment is to teach students a lesson about behavior. Yet published interviews of students regarding suspension and expulsion have found them less likely than adults to believe that discipline keeps them safe and more likely to perceive that school suspension and expulsion are ineffective and unfair. Even students who are most successful within current school structures are likely to criticize school disciplinary policies as meaningless and stultifying. Those students whose behavior does put them at risk for contact with school discipline believe that enforcement is based more on reputation than behavior. Regardless of their own background, most high school students appear to share the perception that school discipline, especially school suspension, unfairly targets poor students and students of color.

FACT: *Students resent arbitrary enforcement of rules and tend to believe that suspension and expulsion are used unfairly against certain groups.*

Perceived Discrimination

ASSUMPTION: *Zero tolerance is more equitable for minorities, since it treats everyone the same.*

Federal education policy prohibits discrimination in the application or outcomes of educational interventions. Yet disciplinary exclusion in general and zero tolerance in particular have consistently led to the disproportionate punishment of students of color. Students of color have consistently been found to be suspended at rates two to three times that of other students, and similarly overrepresented in office referrals, corporal punishment, and school expulsion. If anything, those disparities appear to have increased since the passage of the Gun Free Schools Act. Statistical analyses have shown that racial disparities in school discipline cannot be accounted for by the economic status of minority students; nor is there evidence that minority students misbehave to a degree that would warrant higher rates of punishment. Rather, available data make a case that the use, and especially the overuse, of disciplinary removal carries with it an inherent risk of racial bias.

FACT: Increased use of zero tolerance only seems to increase the disproportionality of African American students in school discipline.

Alternatives to Zero Tolerance

ASSUMPTION: Regardless of the negative effects of suspension and expulsion, there are simply no alternatives to zero tolerance, suspension, and expulsion.

It is probably true that there is a connection between the use of zero tolerance and the belief that there is no alternative. It is most likely the case that schools who believe they must resort to zero tolerance probably do so simply because they believe they have no other choice.

Yet as we learn more about school violence prevention, we have discovered that there are numerous effective alternatives for preserving the safety and integrity of the school learning climate. Educators, researchers, and policymakers have increasingly coalesced around a three-tiered prevention model for improving school safety. That is, at the first level, the school implements programs such as Life Skills or Conflict Resolution on a school-wide basis to promote a positive climate that teaches all students alternatives to disruption and violence. At the second level, programs such as Anger Management are targeted for students who may be at risk for disruption or aggression. Finally, a variety of effective and planned responses are in place to address the issues raised by students who are already engaged in disruptive behavior.

Consistently, programs that effectively cut violence are proactive rather than reactive; involve families, students, and the community; and include multiple components that can effectively address the complexity of school disruption. While it would be overwhelming and probably counter-productive to implement all of the programs . . . , effective schools assess their own needs and choose those strategies and interventions that can best meet those local needs.

FACT: A wide range of alternatives to zero tolerance has emerged and is available to promote a productive learning climate and address issues of disruptive behaviors in the schools.

Effectiveness of Prevention

ASSUMPTION: *Prevention sounds good, but we lack data on its effectiveness and it takes too long to work.*

[Since 1994] there have been numerous studies, including some sponsored by Congress, the U.S. Surgeon General, the Centers for Disease Control, and the Departments of Education, on the most effective methods for preventing youth violence. None of those reports has identified zero tolerance as an effective method for reducing youth violence. Rather, programs that are identified as effective or promising include elements such as bullying prevention, conflict resolution, improved teacher training in classroom management, parent involvement, anger management, and multi-agency collaboration.

Using highly rigorous experimental criteria, these programs have in fact been shown to be far more effective than disciplinary removal in addressing violence and disruption. Further, these types of comprehensive and preventive programs appear to be able to work in a surprisingly short period of time. One program in an inner-city school with high minority dropout rates was able to reduce suspension by 35% in one year by implementing more positive classroom management practices. . . . In Indiana, the Safe and Responsive Schools Project worked with schools in urban, suburban, and rural school districts to develop comprehensive school safety programs. Within one year, the majority of schools showed substantial improvements in both the number and type of school suspensions. . . .

FACT: *Our best data on school violence support preventive strategies as being most likely to ensure school safety. Further, it appears that such programs can have an effect on student behavior and school climate in a surprisingly short period of time.*

Zero Tolerance Is Not Effective

As noted at the outset, educators have the responsibility to use all effective tools at their disposal to maintain the safely and integrity of the school learning climate. There are clearly student behaviors and situations in which the safety of students and teachers demands that certain students be removed from school for a given period of time through suspension or expulsion. Both state law and common sense demand that administrators have the latitude to make those difficult decisions. . . .

Unfortunately, despite almost 15 years of implementation in some of America's schools, there are virtually no data supporting the effectiveness of zero tolerance. Federal zero tolerance policy on weapons seems to have improved consistency of definition in that area. Beyond that, however, there are no data showing that zero tolerance can ensure school safety and improve student behavior. Indeed, the weight of the evidence suggests that zero tolerance suspensions and expulsions are applied too inconsistently to have a positive effect, that they create racial disparities, and that they are associated with negative outcomes in student behavior, school dropout, and academic achievement. Simply put, school suspension and expulsion cannot be viewed as risk-free procedures.

Knowing that a procedure carries certain risks does not mean it should not be used. In the field of medicine, procedures like heart surgery or radiation therapy carry fairly high levels of risk, but are clearly indicated for certain patients. It is also true however, that such procedures are clearly the last medical resort, to be used only after all other alternatives have been exhausted. The problem with the zero tolerance philosophy may not be simply that it increases the use of school suspension and expulsion, but that it may encourage the use of those procedures as a first line of treatment, before other alternatives have been tried. In a recent survey of secondary teachers on school discipline issues, most supported zero tolerance policies for serious behaviors such as drugs and weapons, and thought their schools were adequately responding to these threats. But teachers also believed that if zero tolerance is used as a "blind application of the rules" and without "common sense," the learning climate and their students will suffer.

FOUR

Zero Tolerance Policies Have Produced Mixed Results

Tim Grant

Tim Grant is a reporter for the *Pittsburgh Post-Gazette*. In the following viewpoint, Grant focuses on the implementation of zero tolerance policies in Pennsylvania schools. He presents statistics that show the uneven implementation of zero tolerance policies in schools and cites cases of overly rigid zero tolerance that has been taken to extremes. Grant summarizes the opinions of those who support zero tolerance policies in schools as well as the objections raised by opponents of such policies. Even the strongest supporters of zero tolerance policies in schools admit the difficulty of defining threats and implementing the policies fairly. Most agree that zero tolerance policies should be impartial but flexible enough to allow a commonsense evaluation of each specific incident.

Remember the 10-year-old expelled last school year [2005–2006] from Dible Elementary School in Penn Hills [Pennsylvania] for taking a paintball gun to show-and-tell? What about the seventh-grader at Huston Middle School in Westmoreland County [Pennsylvania] suspended for chewing caffeine energy gum and sharing it with another classmate? Or the 5-year-old boy suspended from kindergarten eight years ago in Deer Lakes

School District [Pennsylvania] for wearing a firefighter costume equipped with a toy ax? Cases like these have become far more common because of zero-tolerance policies that schools across the country have adopted in response to growing concerns about drug use and violence.

Concerns About Zero Tolerance Policies in Schools

"The concern comes when the zero-tolerance policy is so rigid it can't account for some extenuating circumstances," said Tom Hutton, a staff attorney for the National School Boards Association in Alexandria, Virginia. Instead of being reserved for the most serious offenses, suspension, expulsion and criminal court referrals are now common reactions to student misconduct that used to be dealt with in school.

Triggered in part by the Columbine High School shooting in April 1999 [in Colorado] that left 15 people dead, local zero-tolerance policies are born from state and federal laws that give school administrators little leeway in punishing students for behavior that is covered, such as bringing weapons to school, using drugs or alcohol, or making threats. Over the years, some courts have intervened in cases in which school zero-tolerance policies were thought to be too harsh or had somehow violated the constitutional rights of students. "Generally speaking, courts don't want to second-guess a school system," Mr. Hutton said. "Judges don't want to overrule schools left and right. But they will step in when there's a question of whether due process was met."

In *Seal v. Morgan*, a court case involving a school district in Tennessee, a student who was expelled in 2000 based on a zero-tolerance policy when a friend's knife was found in his car's glove compartment complained that the board expelled him without considering whether he knew the knife had been placed there. The board argued that the district was compelled to expel the student whether he knew the knife was there or not. The 6th U.S. Circuit Court of Appeals ruled that a school board "may not absolve itself of its obligation, legal and moral, to determine whether students intentionally committed the acts for which their expulsions are sought by hiding behind a zero-tolerance policy that purports to make the students' knowledge a non-issue."

Too Much Police Involvement?

Locally, court officials are seeing more cases that used to be handled in school systems. "In the 1960s, things like smoking in the boy's bathroom were dealt with by the vice principal," said District Judge David Barton of Baldwin Township [Pennsylvania]. "Now it's a criminal offense." Judge Barton said fights used to be handled at school. Now the school calls police. Police conduct an investigation and cite the participants, resulting in fines and court costs of up to $426.50. If the students are at least 18 years old, fighting at school could lead to a 90-day jail sentence, he said.

District Judge Blaise Larotonda of Mt. Lebanon [Pennsylvania] has mixed feelings on schools using zero tolerance. "It limits your capability to handle each case individually, which is what you need to do, and as a judge we do all the time," he said. "Zero tolerance is a good concept because you have to send that message, but sometimes you can't afford that limitation."

Schools adopt zero-tolerance policies to allow administrators to impose serious penalties for even minor violations to reinforce the overall importance of following the rules. "You have to have policies of this nature so that kids can come to school and feel safe," said John Thomas, superintendent of Aliquippa School District [Pennsylvania]. "We have to give parents reassurance that schools will not tolerate inappropriate behavior that will disrupt teaching and learning." While Mr. Thomas supports zero-tolerance policies, he also believes there are times when the spirit of the law may not be in harmony with the letter of the law. "Sometimes you have to look at the infraction and use your good sense of judgment," he said.

Positive and Negative Results

The increasing use of zero-tolerance policies has yielded positive and negative results. Some students who blatantly violate school

Should All Schools Adopt a Zero Tolerance Policy Toward Any Type of Violence?

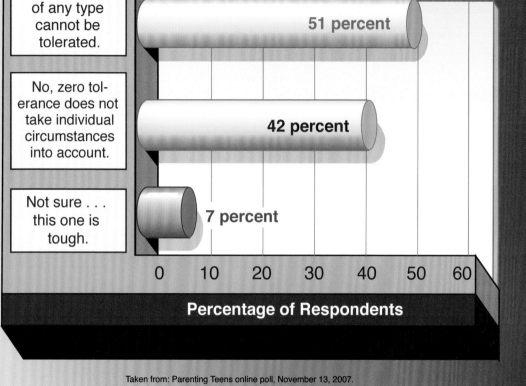

Yes, violence of any type cannot be tolerated. 51 percent

No, zero tolerance does not take individual circumstances into account. 42 percent

Not sure . . . this one is tough. 7 percent

Percentage of Respondents

Taken from: Parenting Teens online poll, November 13, 2007.

rules against weapons, drugs and alcohol are punished before they cause harm or disrupt the learning environment. But sometimes a child with an otherwise clean record is expelled from school, suspended or sent to a detention facility to take classes with chronic offenders. Records provided by the Allegheny County [Pennsylvania] Probation Department show that the vast majority of students that public, charter and private school districts refer to the court system are African-American. Of the 555 students who ended up under court supervision last school year, between September and June, 463 were black and 90 were white, said Jim Rieland, director of Allegheny County probation. "Our intent is not to have zero tolerance, but to keep a kid in school and figure out what the problem is," Mr. Rieland said, adding that he believes the most troubling trend his department found during that nine-month period is more students assaulting teachers.

Most offenses involved weapons on school property. But the law doesn't confine weapons to guns and knives. One child was punished for using a bookbag to beat another student, Mr. Rieland said. Other common offenses include simple assaults and drug charges. "I don't think citizens on the street would call any of these minor offenses," Mr. Rieland said. "These are offenses we should be concerned about. But over the years the trend is flat. I don't think we are getting any more or less in a substantial way." A recent school safety report released by the Pennsylvania Department of Education shows that during the 2004–05 school year, school violence declined for the second year in a row statewide. There were significant decreases in fights, assaults on students, burglaries, racial and ethnic intimidation and incidents involving firearms.

In the past decade, every state has adopted a zero-tolerance law that orders districts to expel for at least one year students who bring guns to school. The measures comply with the 1994 federal gun-free schools law that requires every state to pass such legislation or forfeit federal education aid. There are some loopholes, according to experts. "The law says a superintendent could reduce the punishment and make exceptions," Mr. Hutton said. "But different places have interpreted that law differently."

Witold Walczak, legal director of the American Civil Liberties Union of Pennsylvania, said he thinks rules have to be tempered with common sense to avoid doing harm to children who don't deserve it. "Ultimately, common sense has to come into play," he said. "Zero tolerance eliminates common sense and it doesn't account for unusual circumstances that would counsel mercy or leniency." Mr. Walczak represents the family of Cory Johnson, who was suspended last year from New Brighton High School in Beaver County after students ridiculed him by calling him

"Osama bin Laden" and he reacted in frustration, saying that if he were bin Laden, he would have "pulled a Columbine" by now. "School districts need to understand when they overreact in these situations they do as much harm as when they don't react quickly enough," Mr. Walczak said.

During a 2002 press conference in Bedford, Texas, Gene Buinger, superintendent of the Hurst-Euless-Bedford School District, answers questions about the district's zero tolerance policy toward weapons.

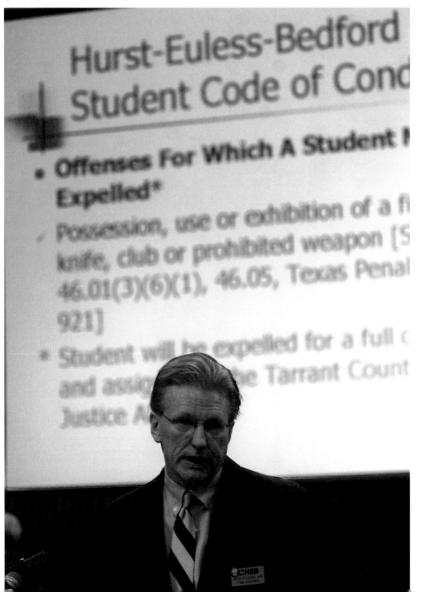

No Consensus

People who support zero-tolerance policies believe they promote safety in schools and give everyone involved more peace of mind. Those who oppose the policies believe they lack rationale and logic and are way too extreme for schools. Members of the Texas Federation of Teachers are trailblazers on the issue of zero tolerance. The organization helped pass the Safe Schools Act in 1995, which outlines circumstances under which a child can be removed from school for interfering with instruction. "We helped invent the term 'zero tolerance' long ago, but unfortunately over time it's gotten convoluted," said Rob D'Amico, spokesman for the federation. "Our position is we want the law followed. That doesn't mean if a child brings fingernail clippers to school we have to expel them," he said. "Unfortunately, some administrators make decisions that are outside the scope of the law and they don't use common sense."

FIVE

Zero Tolerance Policies Are Unfair

Susan Black

Susan Black is an education research consultant and contributing editor of the *American School Board Journal*. In the following viewpoint, Black argues that zero tolerance policies in many schools are discriminatory. Black gives examples from published studies that show racial minority and low-income students are far more likely to be disciplined under zero tolerance policies than other students. Zero tolerance policies remove too many students from schools and yet have not resulted in fewer student behavior problems.

Do zero-tolerance policies make schools safe? Many educators seem to think so—and see zero tolerance as the backbone of school discipline.

One proponent is Patrick Ewing of the State University of New York at Buffalo. Although he admits that some schools have "wildly overreacted" to such minor offenses as drawing pictures of weapons or carrying over-the-counter cold medicine, he believes sensible zero-tolerance policies make schools safer and more secure.

Zero tolerance protects law-abiding students and staff members by allowing for the swift and easy removal of dangerous students,

Ewing says. And it acts as a deterrent to bad behavior by demonstrating swift and serious consequences for defying school rules.

Gerald Tirozzi, executive director of the National Association of Secondary School Principals, agrees. "Zero-tolerance policies are altogether appropriate in the continuing effort to protect students and staff," he says.

Like Ewing, he recognizes that some schools have adopted "imperfect policies" that result in "excessive penalties."

Instead, Tirozzi recommends a "cautious and balanced approach."

- Include parents and community residents in developing policies.
- Explain policies clearly to avoid misinterpretation and misuse.
- Administer policies fairly and consistently, making sure that punishment is age appropriate and fits the offense.
- Ensure due process for accused students.
- Provide suspended or expelled students with alternative educational services and counseling.
- Ensure that discipline regulations in the Individuals with Disabilities Education Act (IDEA) are followed for students with special needs.
- Collect, analyze, and disaggregate student discipline data regularly.
- Review zero-tolerance policies and practices annually.

Unfair Discipline

But many dispute the assumptions that support zero tolerance. Schools that follow Tirozzi's advice are few and far between, according to Ruth Zweifler, executive director of the Student Advocacy Center of Michigan, who says stringent zero-tolerance policies "identify every child as potentially dangerous."

On the surface, Zweifler says, the policies appear sensible and logical, but they end up punishing many children who are "often frightened, sometimes thoughtless, but rarely dangerous."

A 2000 study conducted by the American Educational Research Association (AERA) confirms her assessment. Zero tolerance discipline assumes that school punishment is a "rational act that

Taylor Hess, a 16-year-old honors student at L.D. Bell High School, is pictured at his home in Bedford, Texas. In 2002, Hess was expelled from the school after a knife was found in the bed of his pickup truck.

follows disruptive student behavior in a logical sequence," AERA researchers say, but the sequence is seldom linear.

And it's far from evenhanded: The AERA study found that suspensions and expulsions—the far limits of zero-tolerance discipline—are disproportionately applied to racial minority and low-income students.

The numbers are incriminating. In their 2001 report *Zero Tolerance: Unfair, with Little Recourse*, Dan Losen and Johanna Wald of Harvard University's Civil Rights Project and Judith Browne, senior attorney at the Advancement Project, report that although black students make up only 17 percent of all U.S. students, they account for 33 percent of all out-of-school suspensions and 31 percent of all expulsions. By contrast, 63 percent of all students are white, but they account for only 50 percent of out-of-school suspensions. What's more, the Civil Rights Project reports, students of color are more likely than white students to be suspended or expelled for willful acts, often labeled as disobedience, disruption, or disrespect for authority.

This undercurrent of racial bias has also been noted by Beverly Cross, an urban education specialist at the University of Wisconsin-Madison. "Racism rests just beneath the surface of zero-tolerance decisions," says Cross, who contributed to a 2001 study of racial profiling and punishment in U.S. public schools published by the Applied Research Center's ERASE Initiative. Zero tolerance has created many rule-bound "maximum security schools" where students of color are suspended and expelled at increasing rates, she says, often for nonviolent and subjectively defined offenses.

A case in point is 16-year-old black student who recently told me he'd been expelled from his high school for insubordination. He wasn't sure what the term meant, but he thought it had something to do with "refusing to sit and copy pages out of a ninth-grade science book."

Investigating the matter, I found that his version of events was accurate. I also learned that students in the low-track group, mainly minorities, spent most of their class time filling in worksheets using outdated and dilapidated science books, while those in the high-track group, almost exclusively white, had new books, science labs, and field trips.

This young man was lucky enough to land in a caring, supportive alternative school where the principal and teachers are determined to see him through. But many aren't so fortunate. Vincent Schiraldi, executive director of the Center on Juvenile and Criminal Justice, points out that, under zero tolerance, many kids—especially African-American males—begin a long, hopeless journey into the school-to-prison pipeline.

Has Zero Tolerance Failed?
Zero-tolerance policies are designed to safeguard schools by removing violent students quickly before a bad situation escalates.

Only 17 percent of U.S. students are African American . . .

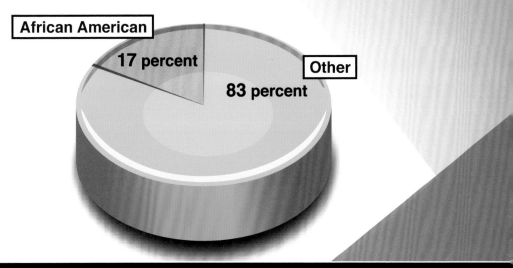

African American

17 percent

Other

83 percent

Total Student Population

. . . but the suspension/expulsion rate of African American students nationwide is 32 percent.

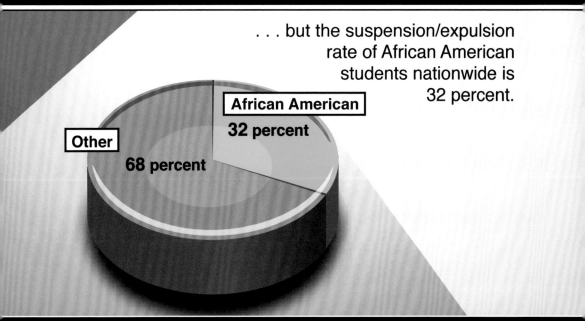

African American

32 percent

Other

68 percent

Student Suspensions/Expulsions

Taken from: Christopher G. Robbins, "Zero Tolerance and the Politics of Racial Injustice," *Journal of Negro Education*, Winter 2005.

But Russell Skiba, director of the Safe and Responsive Schools Project at Indiana University, calls zero tolerance a "simplistic and politically popular" strategy—"a failed experiment that contributes to negative outcomes, including poor school climate and higher rates of delinquency."

The 2001 text *Zero Tolerance: Resisting the Drive for Punishment* reaches the same conclusion. The editors—Rick Ayers, from California's Berkeley High school, William Ayers, of the University of Illinois, and Bernadine Dohrn, at Northwestern University's School of Law—say the "first casualties" of zero tolerance are the "central and critical relationships" between teachers and students and between schools and communities.

The intolerance that results from zero tolerance fails to teach students traits such as understanding, kindness, generosity, benevolence, and justice, William Ayers and Dohrn say. They recommend that schools allow students who've committed relatively minor infractions chances to "grow beyond their transgressions" through a "context of learning" that emphasizes fair treatment and opportunities to change for the better.

Zero tolerance is now the rule in more than 80 percent of the nation's schools. But school district policies are often implemented haphazardly and fail to achieve the major goals of improving students' behavior and ensuring their safety.

Florida's Clearwater High School learned that zero tolerance alone won't solve schoolwide discipline problems. Four years ago, Clearwater replaced its zero-tolerance policies with a graduated discipline system that reserves the most severe consequences for the worst offenses. The school also instituted counseling to help troubled students defuse potentially volatile situations, especially those involving bullying and other aggressive behaviors.

Since the change, Clearwater has cut its suspension rate by 65 percent—and has lowered the dropout rate, reduced the number of classroom disruptions, and raised overall student achievement.

Mixed Lessons

Elsewhere, the lessons from zero tolerance have been mixed. A wave of state laws on zero tolerance was set off after Congress passed the Gun-Free Schools Act of 1994, which ordered states receiving federal funds to pass legislation requiring schools to expel, for a minimum of one year, students who bring firearms to school.

The Tennessee legislature passed such a law, and several Tennessee school boards exercised their option to make their zero-tolerance policies tougher than the state law.

The Knox County school board, for one, added numerous additional offenses, but the board changed its policy after a high school senior, expelled when a friend left a knife in his car, committed suicide [six years later]. The 6th U.S. Circuit Court of Appeals ruled that the expulsion was "irrational" absent evidence that the student knew about the knife. Today, Knox County's policy is to determine appropriate punishment on a case-by-case basis.

In a report on zero tolerance statewide, Kim Potts of Tennessee's Office of Education Accountability examined data for three school years, from 1999 to 2002. According to her August 2003 report:

- Zero-tolerance offenses have increased at a significantly faster rate than student enrollment, rising 10.85 percent from 3,651 in 1999–2000 to 4,047 in 2002-02. In the same time, the number of students enrolled in the state's public schools rose by only 0.68 percent.
- Less than 1 percent of all Tennessee public school students committed zero-tolerance offenses.
- The majority of zero-tolerance offenses involved drugs.
- Ninth-graders were three times more likely to commit a zero-tolerance offense than students in other grades.
- More than half of all offenders were returned to school or placed in alternative schools. Superintendents invoked their option to modify penalties for about 15 percent of offenses.
- African-American students and special education students were overrepresented among zero-tolerance offenders. Boys consistently accounted for some 75 percent of offenses.

The report stops short of calling Tennessee's approach to zero tolerance a failure but says a successful policy "should result in yearly decreases in zero-tolerance violations." It also draws attention to the unintended consequences of zero-tolerance policies— especially the discriminatory use of discipline and the possibility that, in some schools, administrators and teachers use the policies to get rid of troubled and difficult students.

Zero Tolerance Policies Are Unjust

Schools don't need zero-tolerance policies to be safe and secure, says Ellen Boylan, a lawyer with the Education Law Center in Newark, N.J. She reminds school officials that even without such policies, they have the legal right to "remove dangerous and overly disruptive students"—including those who carry guns or other weapons, sell or use illegal drugs, or commit assault.

Boylan advises school boards to consider the procedural protections guaranteed to students by the due process clause of the 14th Amendment. Students assigned to long-term suspension or expulsion must be given notice of the charges and a hearing at which they may present evidence and challenge board witnesses. Special education students have additional rights under IDEA that may prohibit or limit suspension or expulsion under zero-tolerance policies.

A few months ago, I saw Martin Luther King Jr.'s words framed in a high school principal's office: "Injustice anywhere threatens justice everywhere." Those words are worth keeping in mind when it comes to school discipline policies.

SIX

Zero Tolerance Policies Can Be Made Fair

David L. Stader

David L. Stader is a consulting editor for the *Clearing House*, a bimonthly journal of best practices for teachers and school administrators, and an assistant professor at the University of Texas-Arlington. Stader discusses the good and bad aspects of school zero tolerance policies in the following viewpoint. Stader gives examples of the varying results achieved through the use of zero tolerance policies, and concedes that policies have sometimes been implemented unfairly. He argues, however, that zero tolerance policies can be applied fairly, and that student behavior problems can be evaluated on a case-by-case basis to make sure violations and penalties are judged rationally. Stader concludes that schools and students can benefit from balanced zero tolerance policies.

The 1994 Gun-Free Schools Act (GFSA) requires a minimum one-year expulsion for students who bring firearms to school. Although GFSA is not a zero-tolerance law, many school policies enacted in response to GFSA are often referred to as "zero tolerance." Zero tolerance generally is defined as a school district policy that mandates predetermined consequences or punishment for specific offenses, regardless of the circumstances, disciplinary history, or age of the student involved. By 1997, more than 90 percent of public schools reported having zero tolerance policies. In other words, zero tolerance has become public policy. A review of the impact of GFSA and the resultant zero-tolerance policies yields a mixed bag of good, bad, and ugly news.

Good News About Zero Tolerance

The discipline problems public school principals most often cited as serious or moderate problems are student tardiness (40 percent), student absenteeism (25 percent), and fighting between students (21 percent). Weapons, drug sales on campus, and physical assaults on teachers are relatively minor or less prevalent problems; less than 2 percent of the public school principals ranked them as serious or moderate problems in their schools. These findings also are supported by GFSA data. Although any incident of weapons in school is one too many, GFSA data indicate that weapons in schools are relatively rare. For example, in 1999–2000, approximately forty-nine million students attended public schools. Of these, 2,857, or .058 out of 1000, were caught possessing a weapon on campus.

Additional nationwide data support these findings:

- In 1995, 9 percent of students ages 12–18 sometimes or most of the time feared attack or harm at school. In 1999, this percentage had fallen to 5 percent.
- Between 1993 and 1999, the percentage of students in grades 9–12 reporting carrying a weapon on school property within the previous thirty days fell from 12 percent to 7 percent. The percentage of students who reported carrying weapons anywhere during this time period decreased from 22 percent to 17 percent.
- Between 1995 and 1999, the percentage of students ages 12–18 who avoided one or more places at school, citing safety concerns, decreased from 9 percent to 5 percent.

GFSA allows local school administrators to modify (for example, shorten) any disciplinary action for a firearm violation on a case-by-case basis. The primary purpose of this provision is to allow school

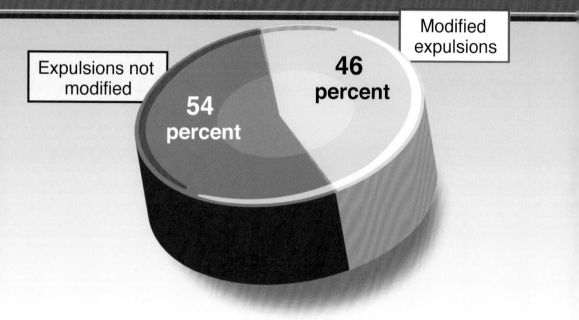

Percentage of School Expulsions Modified in 2003–2004

The national Gun-Free Schools Act allows some flexibility in student discipline, specifically allowing administrators to modify the duration or other details of school expulsions.

Expulsions not modified
54 percent

Modified expulsions
46 percent

Taken from: *Report on Implementation of the Gun-Free Schools Act in the States and Outlying Areas, School Year 2003–2004*, U.S. Department of Education, April 2007.

district administrators and/or boards of education to take the circumstances of the infraction into account and, if necessary, ensure that the legal requirements of the Individuals with Disabilities Education Act (IDEA) are honored. GFSA data indicate that school districts are taking advantage of this option. . . .

The Courts Get Involved

Courts generally are supportive of reasonable zero-tolerance policies designed to improve school safety. For example, in a high-profile 2001 case, six students were involved in a violent fight in the stands of a high school football game in Decatur, Illinois. The district, citing gang-like activities, physical violence, and endangerment policies, expelled the offending students for two years. After national publicity and political pressure, the board modified the two-year suspensions to two semesters and made an alternative school placement possible. Still dissatisfied, the expelled students sought a court order reinstating them. The students claimed that they had been deprived of procedural due process, subjected to racial discrimination, and that the district's "gang-like activity" policy was void for vagueness. The Seventh Circuit summarily rejected all three claims, finding that the students had received adequate due process, a lack of evidence that the students had been treated disparately on the basis of race, and the provisions of the district's discipline policy dealing with gangs were constitutionally sound.

In a few notable cases, courts have brought some semblance of reason to the table. For example, in *Seal v. Morgan* (2000), Dustin Seal brought action against the Knox County (Tennessee) Board of Education for expelling him from high school after a friend's knife was found in the glove compartment of his car. Seal denied any knowledge of the knife's presence in the car while it was on school property and argued that the school board's action was irrational. Although it recognized that not expelling a dangerous student carries significant consequences for all concerned, the court held that consistency is not a substitute for rationality and that the application of a zero-tolerance policy in this particular case was indeed irrational. A school board may not absolve itself of its legal and moral obligation to determine whether students intentionally committed the acts for which they were expelled by hiding behind a zero-tolerance policy that makes the student's knowledge a nonissue. The District Court of New Mexico took a similar position when a senior student was expelled despite a hearing officer's finding that the student unknowingly had brought weapons to school when he borrowed his brother's car.

Bad News About Zero Tolerance

The accuracy of the current GFSA data is questionable. . . . GFSA data report on only those students caught with a weapon in school. . . . Other data indicate that substantially more students carried a weapon to school than the expulsion data of GFSA indicate. In addition, after two years of declining numbers, 2000–2001 data indicated a 29 percent increase. However, the number of modified expulsions increased from 27 percent to 42 percent. Assuming that the expulsion of a truly dangerous student would not be modified, the data may indicate that the increase in the number of weapons in school may translate into better reporting methods rather than an increased danger.

Although there is little ambiguity regarding the expulsion of truly dangerous students, some school district applications of zero-tolerance policies cast doubt on the wisdom of school administrators. For example, a threatening letter was found a few days after the 1999 Columbine attacks in a computer lab in Brazosport (Texas) High School. School administrators suspected a particular student. The local police department confronted, frisked, handcuffed, and led fourteen students (presumably including the suspected student) who "hung out" together out of the school building and transported them to the local municipal court, where the police and the school principal hastily lectured the students and their parents. The next day, the school principal called a school-wide assembly to explain the prior day's happenings and to pronounce the school "free of terrorists." Several of the lectured students suffered sleepless nights, agitation, and fatigue from harassment by other students. When parents confronted the principal, he suggested that the affected students could either transfer or begin home schooling. However, the District Court for Southern Texas pointed out that the authoritative actions must have been effective since no violent act came to fruition at the high school.

In October 1999, Benjamin Ratner (then in the eighth grade) was told by a female friend that she had considered suicide by slitting her wrists the previous evening. She informed Benjamin that she inadvertently had brought a knife to school in her binder that morning. Benjamin knew the student and was aware of her previous suicide attempts. He put the binder in his locker with the intent of telling both his and her parents after school. School officials obtained knowledge of the knife. When confronted, Benjamin voluntarily went unescorted to his locker and gave the binder willingly to the dean of students. The dean acknowledged that Benjamin acted in what he saw as the girl's best interest and at no time posed a threat to himself or anyone else.

Nevertheless, Benjamin was suspended for ten days for possessing a knife on school grounds. He was notified two days later that he was being suspended indefinitely pending further action by the school board. An administrative hearing panel recommended that Benjamin be suspended for the remainder of the school year. On judicial appeal, the Fourth Circuit Court refused to consider Benjamin's case, finding he had been given constitutionally sufficient, even if imperfect, due process. In addition, the court expressed an unwillingness to judge the wisdom of the zero-tolerance policy legally adopted by a local board of education.

In a concurring opinion in *Ratner*, Judge Hamilton questioned the wisdom of the decision by stating, "Each (Benjamin, his family, and common sense) is the victim of good intentions run amuck." It is easy to find fault in Benjamin's choice not to give his friend's binder to a principal, counselor, or trusted teacher. It is also easy to defend the Brazosport (Texas) principal's concern about a threatening note the day after Columbine. However, when do actions to promote school safety transcend common sense and, rather than make schools safer, promote a kind of distrust that deters future reporting?

Racial Inequality in Zero Tolerance Implementation

Few racial or ethnic differences exist in the percentages of students carrying weapons anywhere on school property. Yet, students of color are more likely to be suspended than white students. In a study of suspension and expulsion data from twelve cities, researchers found that in the eleven cities in which disaggregate data were available, African American and Latino students were suspended or expelled at a significantly higher proportional rate than white students. For example, in Austin, Texas, 18 percent of the student population is African American, 43 percent is Latino, and 37 percent is white. African American students accounted for 36 percent of the suspensions and expulsions, Latino students for 45 percent, and white students for 18 percent. A similar pattern is apparent in the other ten cities from which disaggregate data were available.

Unfortunately, the pattern found by Gordon, Piana, and Keleher may not be unique. The students in *Fuller v. Decatur* (2000) alleged that the Decatur school district maintained a practice of arbitrary and disparate expulsions with regard to African American students. The district court ordered the Decatur school administrators to produce expulsion records for the past two years disaggregated by race. African American students comprise 46 to 48 percent of the student body in the Decatur school district. The summary data indicated that 82 percent of the students expelled during this period were African American. The remaining 18 percent were white.

The problem is not with the Decatur school district's decision to expel the students involved in the fight at the football game. These students should have been suspended regardless of their race, sex, or ethnicity. The issue is with the need for awareness and training to confront possible disproportional suspension and expulsion rates. For example, administrators in the Decatur school district apparently had not considered the disproportional number of African American students referred for expulsion before forced to do so by the district court. As Amanda Lewis points out, "[T]alk about race [is] dangerous: [schools] could be accused of failing, could be accused of racism, could be forced to confront realities that contradict the racially liberal narrative that frames [the] profession." But these concerns should not justify ignoring the suspension or expulsion of students of color at a significantly higher proportional rate than their fellow white students.

Achieving Balance

School safety is important. The failure to remove a dangerous student from a school is a great risk to students and faculty. At the same time, the misapplication of suspension/expulsion authority carries significant consequences for some students (such as Benjamin) who pose little threat to school safety. As the Sixth Circuit Court points out, consistency may not always be rational. The problem is deciding when rationality should outweigh consistency.

[Some experts] argue that student expulsion decisions often are not only a product of student behavior but also are driven by the educational philosophy, policies, and practices of the particular school system. They assume that schools with more student-centered and flexible discipline practices would expel fewer students. Therefore, flexible policies that provide a range of alternatives that take into consideration the circumstances surrounding a situation may be advisable. This assumption is supported by . . . a U.S. Secret Service report on threat assessment in schools. This report recommends that decisions should focus on the totality of behaviors, motives, and communications rather than relying on a single one-size-fits-all policy. . . .

[The authors] acknowledge that efforts to assess the level of threat require the exercise of some common sense. Common sense . . . means to step back and ask if the information supports any hypothesis developed about potential punishment.

In addition, [some experts suggest] that students facing suspension or expulsion for serious infractions be referred to law enforcement and to a community counseling agency for evaluation. Although any incident rated as a moderate to severe threat warrants significant punishment, outside agencies can provide school officials a second and third opinion that further justifies a decision to allow a student to return to school, to be placed in an alternative setting, or to be expelled. For example, a student (like Benjamin) that presents little, if any, threat could receive short-term or in-school suspension. Another similarly circumstanced student who presented a moderate threat and is judged by law enforcement and/or a counseling agency to be at risk of violence may be eligible for expulsion.

Making Zero Tolerance Policies Fair

School leaders have a legal obligation to keep schools safe. They also have an ethical obligation to examine the consequences of their actions and, if necessary, make changes in policy and practice to not only keep schools safe but also to protect individual students from the capricious application of policy. The following recommendations are only a few of the actions that school leaders should consider in finding a balance to their decisions:

1. Collect, analyze, and disaggregate student discipline data. Accurate district data by campus on suspensions or expulsions by offense, race or ethnicity, and sex are mandatory.

Some feel that zero tolerance polices can benefit everyone if developed and implemented correctly.

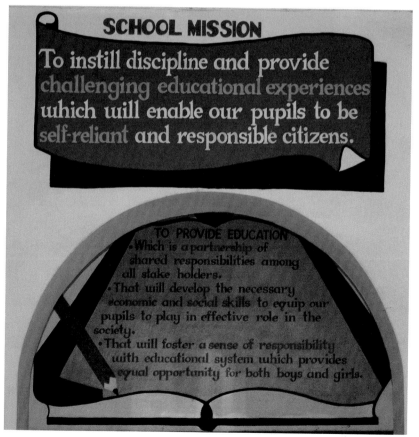

Careful data collection provides much needed information and provides the evidence to support or the catalyst to review current policy and practice. . . .

2. Develop objective criteria to use in suspension/expulsion decisions. Criteria could include factors surrounding the incident, previous behavior of the student, relative severity or threat of the incident, and evidence of school support.

3. Set and annually review qualitative and measurable objectives to reduce the number of suspensions and expulsions and prevent school violence. Objectives should have clearly articulated research/literature-driven interventions that target specific areas of need.

4. Work with students, parents, and community groups to articulate and explain school district policy and practice.

Some evidence suggests that GFSA and the resultant zero-tolerance policies have been effective in reducing weapon possession in school. Zero-tolerance policies have been supported by various courts, especially when the policy is tied to school safety. However, suspensions and expulsions often are a product of student behavior, school policy and, more important, application of school policy. A policy that provides written guidelines that consider several factors may provide the flexibility and defensibility to address not only dangerous students but the less dangerous as well. In other words, zero tolerance has a place—just a balanced place.

SEVEN

Zero Tolerance Policies Harm Students

Whitney Joiner

> Whitney Joiner is an independent journalist and fre-
> quent contributor to the online magazine Salon.com.
> In the following viewpoint, Joiner discusses incidents of
> school zero tolerance policy that have harmed students
> and their families. She gives details about specific cases in
> which unjustified school expulsions have had devastating
> consequences for students and their families. The high
> cost of legal defense alone burdens families who decide
> to fight zero tolerance rulings. Joiner includes interviews
> with parents of several students who were involved in
> such cases.

In November 1996, Dustin Seal, then a high school senior, was expelled after authorities at his Knoxville, Tennessee, high school found a 3-inch knife in his car. Even though the knife wasn't Dustin's, and even though the friend who'd left the knife in Dustin's car claimed responsibility for it, the administration didn't budge: Under the school's "zero tolerance" policy, every student found with a weapon on campus had to be expelled.

Dustin became depressed and withdrawn after his expulsion, says his father, Dennis, a 58-year-old retired commercial contrac-tor. "He would ask me constantly: 'When are they going to let me back in school with my friends? How can they take everything away from me when I've done nothing wrong?'"

The Seals sued the school district and took time case all the way to the Supreme Court, winning at every step. But by the time the Court sent the case back to the local level for Dustin to claim damages, he was too exhausted to continue fighting. He settled for $30,000 in December of 2001.

Six months later, Dustin spent a June day with his father shooting pool. He went home that night and repeatedly left messages on Dennis's answering machine while Dennis, sick in bed, slept in the next room: "It doesn't look like we're going to the bike show tomorrow, Dad, but I love you." "Dad—goodbye."

Then he drew a bath, got in the bathtub, stuck a pistol under his chin and pulled the trigger. He was 22 years old.

Almost two years after his son's suicide, Dennis Seal is suing the Knox County school board for wrongful death, claiming that Dustin's suicide was a direct result of his expulsion. "It broke his spirit and he never got over it," says Seal. School district spokesman Russ Oaks wouldn't comment on Seal's case, but, he says, "Zero tolerance has helped to ensure a safer school environment." The case goes to trial this October [2004].

Clearing his son's name has consumed Dennis Seal's life. "That's all I've done for two years," he says. He's spent well over $30,000 in legal fees, and is planning to try the case himself, after unsatisfactory experiences with lawyers spurred him to study for a law degree online through a local community college. He says he never received a letter of condolence from the school district.

The Problem with Zero Tolerance

Dennis Seal's story is perhaps the most harrowing example of a zero tolerance policy gone awry—but it's not the only one. A growing number of parents across the country are struggling to deal with their children's expulsions, for what they claim are minor infractions blown out of proportion. According to the National Center for Education Statistics [NCES] a zero tolerance policy is a "school or district policy that mandates predetermined

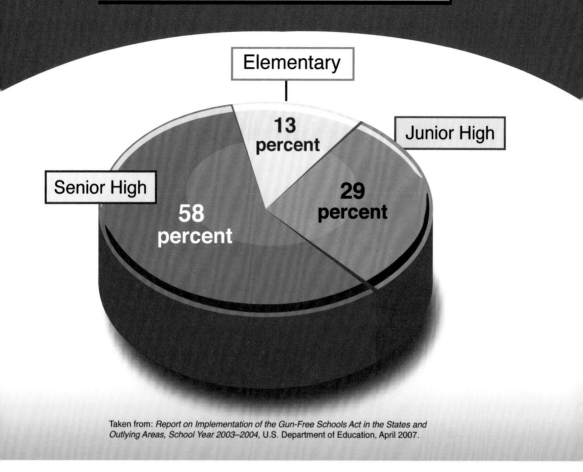

Percentage of Expulsions Nationwide by School Level, 2003–2004

Elementary

13 percent

Junior High

Senior High

58 percent

29 percent

Taken from: *Report on Implementation of the Gun-Free Schools Act in the States and Outlying Areas, School Year 2003–2004*, U.S. Department of Education, April 2007.

consequences or punishments for specific offenses"—which has all too often come to mean that whether the drug is cocaine or cold medicine, whether the weapon is a butter knife or a shotgun, the penalty will be the same. Like the mandatory sentencing laws of the early '90s, which have overcrowded prisons with felons convicted of relatively low-level crimes forced to serve long sentences, zero tolerance is a one-size-fits-all policy, critics say—and treating every offense the same, regardless of the context, just doesn't work.

School officials across the country say that after school shootings at Paducah and Jonesboro, Springfield and Columbine, they can't afford to take chances. And just as no one wants to repeal crime laws for fear of seeming soft on crime, school districts are reluctant to change zero tolerance policies for fear of sending the message that discipline in schools is no longer a priority. About 79 percent of public schools have zero tolerance policies for violence and tobacco and 94 percent for firearms, reports NCES.

News stories of children expelled under zero tolerance abound (the girl who was kicked out of school for writing a violent story in her diary; the boy expelled for lending his asthma inhaler to his asthmatic girlfriend), but what goes unreported is the private suffering endured by families of accused kids: the financial devastation from legal costs and private school tuition; the social isolation, as many must dedicate their time to defending their child; the shame of being seen by the community as a "bad" parent. Worst of all is the emotional toll on the children, who are left with few educational alternatives and deep feelings of anger and betrayal toward a system they've been raised to trust.

Parents affected by zero tolerance are networking through the Web, thanks to sites like EndZeroTolerance.com and e-mail groups like Parents Against Zero Tolerance. Some, like Dennis Seal, have been inspired to take political action—he's running for a school board seat in November [2004]—but most depend on the other parents they meet via the Web for legal advice and, especially, emotional support.

"I feel really close to a number of [the parents]," says Mary LeBlanc, a 51-year-old Louisiana receptionist whose 17-year-old son Adam was expelled, arrested, chained to the wall of a police station by his ankles and thrown in jail after his younger brother's school bus driver found a drawing in a sketch pad that depicted Adam and his friends attacking the high school with ICBM[s] [intercontinental missiles]. "They know exactly where you're coming from and they're very encouraging. It's very difficult to find someone in this community who can sympathize and understand. You find the most comfort from parents who've been through similar things. If I didn't have that, I would've been lost."

Zero Tolerance Policies Don't Work

The Gun-Free Schools Act, [signed] by President Bill Clinton in 1994, mandates a one-year expulsion for any student found with drugs or weapons on campus. The law was designed to protect students from serious dangers, but school boards—the interpreters of the law, since public schools are run at the local level—began to tighten their policies after the mid-'90s spate of school shootings, ushering in the era of zero tolerance. Immediately, suspension and expulsion rates zoomed nationwide. According to the Department of Education's Office of Civil Rights, the total number of suspensions and expulsions for both elementary and secondary schools rose from 1,977,862 in 1990 to 3,150,626 in 2000.

The continuing rapid rise of these numbers prove that zero tolerance doesn't really work, says Russell Skiba, an associate professor in educational psychology at Indiana University and the director of the Safe and Responsive Schools Project, who has just completed two major studies on zero tolerance. "Schools will say, 'We need these policies to keep these schools safe, and if we make any exceptions it'll reduce safety.' The important piece is whether it really is making a contribution to our schools. The best data says it isn't."

Even those charged with carrying out the policies don't necessarily agree with them. "I dislike lumping every single case into one category," says Curt Lavarello, executive director of the National Association of School Resource Officers. ("Resource officer" is the official term for school police officers.) "We know the difference between a kid who has a knife because he's a fisherman and a kid who's going to use the knife to stab his classmates. But when you institute a zero tolerance policy, you have no choice: You become more of a robot in your police work."

So why is expulsion no longer a last resort, and how could anyone suspend a child for something as innocuous as bringing Midol to school? "Parents want to be assured that their children will be safe," says Bill Modzeleski, associate deputy undersecretary for the Office of Safe and Drug-Free Schools at the U.S. Department of Education. "I assume that, yes, with 52 million kids and 15,000 school districts there probably are some policies that some individuals call harsh. But there are other parents who say, 'They're not harsh, because those are the same policies that are protecting my son and daughter.'"

School districts and zero tolerance proponents like Modzeleski say that common sense must prevail—that school boards do take extenuating circumstances into account at expulsion hearings and that all children are offered due process. But for parents trying to keep their children in school, common sense seems like the last thing on the minds of the administrators.

Common Sense Is Needed

Graduate student Howard Hastings, 52, whose 14-year-old son Karel was expelled in 2000 for giving a joint to another child at his Fairfax County, Virginia, middle school, says that during his son's expulsion hearing, an earlier 10-day absence was seen as suspicious and added to the school's proof of Karel's guilt. It didn't matter that the absence was due to a wrestling injury that left Karel—a local wrestling star—unable to walk for over a week.

Hastings was furious with Karel for his marijuana experimentation, he says, and planned to punish him. He immediately met with the school administration and told Karel to be as honest as possible about the joint he'd given his friend, assuming that if they "played by their rules and did everything the school required," Karel might be readmitted. But the administration was determined to expel Karel, says Hastings, and by the time the school's discipline measures added up—mandating that Karel attend multiple Alcoholics Anonymous meetings and group therapy every week on top of expulsion—Hastings felt that the school's punishment was more than enough. In fact, he now wishes that he hadn't pushed Karel to be completely honest with the school.

"If we had to do it all over again, I might've said, 'Just keep silent,'" says Hastings. "We trusted [the school]. We're used to going in and talking to a teacher about how our kid is doing. But they weren't interested in him at all."

Fairfax County School District coordinator of community relations Paul Regnier notes that Karel pled guilty in court to possession of a controlled substance, and that "the school district felt there was evidence of distribution"—which factored into its decision to expel.

Mary LeBlanc, the Louisiana mother whose 17-year-old son Adam was arrested for a drawing, says that when the school found a box cutter on her son, they immediately interpreted it as proof of Adam's dangerous nature—even though she repeatedly told the administration that he needed it at his long-term after-school job at a family-owned grocery store. "They weren't having any part of that," she says. "My son was obviously planning something."

Ascension Parish assistant superintendent Donald Sogny, who wouldn't comment specifically on Adam's case, says that the media only gets half the story. "I'm not going to air a child's dirty laundry," he says. "We can tell you a lot more that might convince you that maybe it wasn't a small thing." He also notes that not every child recommended for expulsion ends up expelled: In fact, two cases in his district last month [January 2004] were "modified significantly," he says.

A Hopeless Situation

"Zero tolerance looks good on paper," says Diane Rohman, 38, whose son was expelled from high school in the same district where she works as a middle school art teacher in Stafford County, Virginia. Rohman estimates that her middle school has already expelled about three students this year—one for carrying over-the-counter cold medicine. "It makes it look like we're doing something to make the schools safe. But I don't think anyone [in the community] is really aware of what it is."

Rohman's 17-year-old son, Anthony, her only child, was expelled on the first day of his senior year in high school last September after administrators found a marijuana seed in the back seat of his car. Rohman claims the seed came from a boy who was riding in the back seat of the car. "They call it due process, but I have never walked into a situation where I felt that nothing I said would've mattered," says Rohman of her son's expulsion hearing. "I knew it was hopeless—appeals never go through. The attorneys

Rev. Jesse Jackson addresses questions during a news conference in 1999. Jackson filed a lawsuit against a Decatur, Illinois, school district after six students were expelled for fighting under their school's zero tolerance policy.

said it was a no-win situation with the school." It seemed especially unjust, she says, "because I'm a colleague of these people. It made me angrier."

As a single parent on a teacher's salary, Rohman couldn't afford private school tuition, and, like many districts, the other public schools in the county wouldn't accept an expelled student. So Rohman sent Anthony to live with her brother in Maryland, four hours away. She visits him every few weeks, but the separation has been tough. "I knew next year that he'd be going away to college," she says, "but when it happens within a week—I just wasn't mentally prepared for it."

The Stafford County Public School District declined to comment on Anthony's case.

Hastings and his wife also sent their son to live with relatives—Karel's grandmother, across the country in Montana—for seven months. As much as they hated the separation from their son, says Hastings, it was better than keeping him in the local alternative school, where, ironically, what was designed as rehabilitation for Karel's "drug problem" ended up putting him at much greater risk. "He was the only little kid there," says Hastings. "Some of those kids were 18, smoking pot behind the building with no supervision." Hastings accompanied his son to school every day, worked on his dissertation at a local library, then drove Karel the 45 minutes back home.

The Cost to Families

Oftentimes, parents' lives are put on hold as they spend months—or years—defending their child. Hastings, a Ph.D. student in cultural studies at George Mason University, still hasn't finished graduate school. "I hoped I could get my dissertation wrapped up in that year, and now I still don't have it," he says. "Almost immediately after Karel's expulsion most of my time was taken up driving him to various things—to appointments with the school, to the mandatory AA meetings and therapy." Setting aside his degree has affected his family's finances, he says. "It's cut our earning power. If I don't have the degree, I can't get the job. And I've had to keep paying tuition."

"At the beginning you think, OK, well, this is going to be an annoyance," says D.C. lawyer Paul Brown, 55, whose 17-year-old learning-disabled son was expelled early in his freshman year. "But it's a two-week suspension and then expulsion and it just goes on and on and on. I thought, well, I'm sure the school will be reasonable—but by the time you realize you should've gotten a lawyer, it's too late."

Brown's son brought a toy gun, and real ammunition, to the bus stop to scare the kids who called him a "fag" on a daily basis. "I would have punished him severely," Brown wrote in an e-mail. But by acting in loco parentis [in the place of a parent], the school superseded Brown's parental decisions. "Since the school came down so hard on him, I had to shift gears to defend my son. He had no other defenders. I went from feeling that parents and teachers were united in educating my son to feeling the school system was the enemy." The district allowed his son into a neighboring public school (he'll graduate this spring [2004]), but only after hiring a personal security guard to escort Brown's son everywhere on campus.

Jeanette Hartwell, 47, moved her entire family from Rancho Cucamonga, California, to the neighboring town of Ontario to live with relatives after her son DJ was expelled from Ruth Musser Middle School for joking with a classmate about opening fire in school with a Glock semiautomatic handgun. The Hartwells shelled out $15,000 in lawyers' fees to fight DJ's expulsion. When the board wouldn't allow DJ to return, the family coughed up an additional $13,000 to pay for private school tuition for DJ and his two younger brothers—fees they couldn't afford on Jeanette's husband's salary as a police officer. The Hartwells were forced to sell the home they'd purchased a year earlier.

"It was a nice house, and we'd just begun to think of it as home," says DJ, now 16. He knew the conversation with his friend was inappropriate, says DJ, a self-described loner who loves books and politics. But "I was kind of starved for any sort of friendly interaction," he says. "So if he wanted to start a conversation about it I wasn't going to stop him. I didn't think it was harmful to anybody." That was the last conversation he had with his friend. After his expulsion, DJ says, "I felt very betrayed and very hurt. I was in shock. I felt very alone."

("We're not going to comment on this," said Cathy Preston, administrative assistant to the superintendent of Central School District in Rancho Cucamonga. "That was a private matter and we don't discuss students.")

The Cost to Students

Besides battling school districts, these parents also struggle to keep their children mentally healthy. As Dustin Seal's case illustrates, expulsion can have a deep effect on a child's emotional state and sense of self. "I see anxiety and depression becoming almost the most powerful things in their lives," says Jerry Wyckoff, a former school psychologist now in private practice in Overland Park, Kansas, who has worked with about 15 children embroiled in zero tolerance cases. "The kids just can't understand why this happened to them. They feel completely, totally wronged. Adolescents have trouble trusting adults anyway, and this just confirms that all adults are against me; there's no one in the world who can help me."

For kids who are both expelled and arrested, finding a way to move on proves especially hard. Since he had a felony on his record, Dustin Seal wasn't able to find a job after his expulsion. "He wanted to be an attorney," says Dennis Seal, "but he couldn't even work at McDonald's."

And since expulsion means that the student is not only barred from school, but from all school events, activities that might have helped the child—sports or clubs that could raise self-esteem or foster positive relationships with other kids—are now off-limits. Hastings' son, the wrestler, was forced off the team since they trained at the local school.

Rohman's son, Anthony, always loved baseball, she says; playing for the school team was his passion. "After he left," she says, "I found his team jersey in the trash in his room. He was so proud of that before [his expulsion]."

For Brown and his wife, who were active school volunteers and supporters, their son's expulsion meant that they ended up ostracized as well. "Once your kid is no longer going to school with other kids, we no longer saw our friends," he says. "We didn't go to the games, we didn't go to the plays. We were totally isolated from people we'd known for years."

"But it's not just the parents who suffer," says Brown. "It's his older brother, too, because you have to focus all your attention on one kid."

Jeanette Hartwell's two younger sons were doing well in the public school when her oldest son, DJ, was expelled. Wary of the public school system, she enrolled them all in private school. "[My middle son] was in the band and played for the school's roller hockey team. He had to leave all that," she says. "It hurt him. He had a lot of friends and was well liked."

While parents like Dennis Seal have thrown themselves into fighting against zero tolerance—Seal says he gets about a call a week from other parents asking for advice—it's been difficult for parents, like Brown, to take any political action toward ending the policies. "It's hard to form a support group of people who hate the school, because you're also ashamed of your status as a parent," he says. "Your kid reflects on you. You go into the school year thinking everything is wonderful and your kid will be educated. Then you find out—oh, my kid is one of those kids who shouldn't be in school at all."

Joining Parents Against Zero Tolerance [PAZT] has made Rohman more politically active, she says. She's attended an academic conference about school discipline with other PAZT members, and she presented a lengthy paper to the school board, arguing against her county's zero tolerance policies. The board agreed to start looking at individual cases instead of doling out the same punishments regardless of the details.

After her success with the board, she says, "I do feel like what you say and do can make a difference." But she's not planning to stick around to find out: After the school year is over, she's considering moving closer to her son and finding another teaching position. "I don't feel like I can stay here after this. I love my school; I love my job. I don't want to leave—but I don't want to stay in a county that would do this to my son."

As for Seal, he's determined to make sure that his son did not die in vain. "I have to have closure," he says. "I don't want anything like this to ever happen again."

EIGHT

Zero Tolerance Policies Violate Students' Right to Privacy

Elisabeth Frost

> Elisabeth Frost is a former editorial staff member at the *Washington Law Review*, a scholarly journal run by students at the University of Washington School of Law in Seattle. In the following viewpoint, Frost argues that zero tolerance policies in schools often violate students' constitutional right to privacy. She summarizes the laws protecting the right to privacy, particularly with regard to possession of certain prescription drugs. Frost also outlines court cases that have established and confirmed students' right to privacy in specific situations. Frost concludes that automatically notifying parents when a student is found to have certain prescription drugs is unconstitutional.

Schools have broadly applied zero tolerance drug policies to a wide range of prescription and non-prescription medication, including items not traditionally considered "medication," such as vitamins and birth control pills. Many zero tolerance drug policies subject a student to discipline, normally without exception, if the school catches her in possession of any kind of medication at school, unless the student previously obtained parental permission to possess that medication. The consequence of that discipline

Elisabeth Frost, "Zero Privacy: Schools Are Violating Students' Fourteenth Amendment Right of Privacy Under the Guise of Enforcing Zero Tolerance Policies," *Washington Law Review*, vol. 81, May 2006, pp. 391–417. Copyright © 2006 University of Washington School of Law. Reproduced by permission.

has included the notification of the student's parents and the general public. Nevertheless, the proponents of these policies argue that zero tolerance policies are in the students' best interests.

Parental Consent

Generally, zero tolerance drug policies that cover prescription and over-the-counter medication allow students to bring legally prescribed or over-the-counter medication to school only if the student provides the school with a doctor's note, parental approval, or both. A representative Ohio school district policy provides that "[a] student shall not knowingly possess[,] . . . consume, use, handle, give, store, [or] conceal . . . any . . . non-prescription or prescription drug (except when under the direction of a physician/parent and within school procedure . . .)." Violation of this policy results in a ten-day suspension and a chemical dependency evaluation. Often, zero tolerance policies do not define "prescription drug," but where definitions are included they can be broad, such as the City of Virginia Beach policy that defines prohibited "medication" as "any drug or other substances used in treating disease, healing, or relieving pain, including all over-the-counter drugs such as aspirin, cough syrups, gargles, caffeine pills and the like." Many zero tolerance policies further forbid students from self-administering or personally possessing medication while on school grounds, requiring that the student leave parentally approved medication for safekeeping with the school nurse.

Parental Notification

Pursuant to zero tolerance drug policies, schools across the country have punished students for possession and use of a variety of substances that, but for the application of zero tolerance policies, would be perfectly legal. For example, schools have severely disciplined students for taking ibuprofen for menstrual cramps, possessing heartburn-relief medicine to control intestinal gas, and sharing zinc cough drops without first clearing the cough drops with the school office. In one particularly egregious example, a school expelled a fourteen-year-old for eighty days for taking Midol for

A police drug dog sniffs out the lockers at Austin High School in Decatur, Alabama, during a random surprise search.

severe menstrual pain and giving Midol to another student. That school's zero tolerance policy provided that "student[s] shall not knowingly possess[,] . . . consume, use, handle, give, store, [or] conceal . . . any . . . non-prescription or prescription drug (except when under the direction of a physician/parent and within school procedure . . .)." District officials later told the punished student that if she and her parent agreed to have her undergo a substance abuse evaluation, the district would remove the expulsion from her school record.

An Oklahoma school district demonstrated that some school administrators include prescription contraception within the scope of zero tolerance drug policies when it suspended a fourteen-year-old for prescription hormone pills found in her purse. Administrators claimed that a district-wide "zero tolerance policy" mandated a one-year suspension for student possession of any "illegal" substance, including cough drops or legally prescribed medication. After the student obtained legal representation, the district agreed to reduce the suspension to five days if the student attended drug counseling and underwent urinalysis. However, the district told the student that her suspension for this possession of an "illegal substance" would remain on her permanent record. The student appealed the decision and eventually, after the involvement of lawyers, a settlement with the district was reached expunging her record.

Keeping Students Safe?

Supporters of zero tolerance policies claim that the purpose of such policies is to protect students. Proponents specifically argue that the policies keep schools safe and have the general support of parents and school officials. In attempting to identify the school's rationale for a policy that resulted in a fourteen-year-old's suspension for giving a friend Midol, a federal district court found that the school's justification for the policy was "the need to protect students who may have adverse reactions to non-prescription medication; the need to control the flow of all substances, legal and illegal, in the public schools; and the need to ensure that even non-prescription drugs are not used in a harmful manner by students." These rationalizations encompass the primary justifications put forth on behalf of zero tolerance proponents.

In sum, schools have broadly applied zero tolerance drug policies to a wide range of medication, including prescription contraceptives. Under such policies, students must obtain parental permission to possess otherwise legal medical contraceptives. Schools have severely disciplined students even for minor violations of these policies—including possession of otherwise legal substances. The effect of such discipline has included notification of students' parents and the general public. Nevertheless, the proponents of zero tolerance policies argue that such policies are in students' best interests.

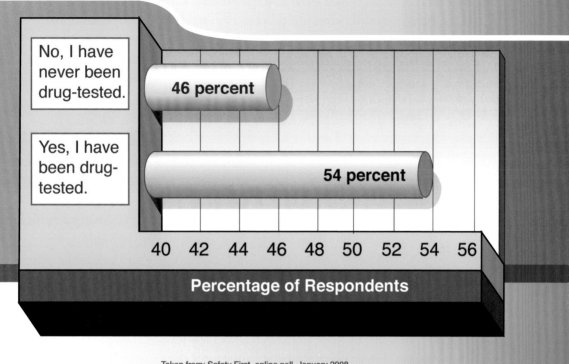

No, I have never been drug-tested.

46 percent

Yes, I have been drug-tested.

54 percent

40 42 44 46 48 50 52 54 56

Percentage of Respondents

Taken from: Safety First, online poll, January 2008.

Violating Students' Policy

Requiring that a student obtain parental consent in order to "legally" possess medical contraceptives at school amounts to a blanket parental consent requirement of the type that the Supreme Court has held to be an unconstitutional violation of a minor's Fourteenth Amendment right of privacy. Also, when a school disciplines a minor under a zero tolerance policy for possessing contraceptives, the discipline unavoidably and unconstitutionally results in parental notification of her contraceptive choices. Disciplining a student for possessing contraceptives also often results in unconstitutional dissemination of the student's private affairs to the public. Moreover, none of the rationalizations proffered in support of such policies amount to a significant state interest justifying interference in a minor's procreative decision-making.

School policies that forbid students from possessing contraceptives without parental consent effectively compel students to obtain third-party consent in order to exercise their constitutionally protected right to make contraceptive choices. If a minor is required to obtain parental consent in order to avoid violating such a policy, the parent may choose to withhold consent, resulting in an unconstitutional arbitrary veto. In the alternative, a student who does not wish to risk violating the policy, but also does not wish to inform her parents of her contraceptive choices, may instead choose to stop using contraceptives, despite her constitutional right to choose to do so.

Even if a student avoids parental consent by choosing to risk violating a zero tolerance policy, disciplining a student caught with medical contraceptives in violation of a zero tolerance policy has the impermissible result of notifying the minor's parents of her contraceptive choices. This unavoidable parental notification unconstitutionally interferes with a minor's Fourteenth Amendment right of privacy. Notification, or the threat thereof, is likely to result in severe infringement of students' contraceptive-related decision-making. Such notification through punishment is also at odds with the Court's holding regarding recordkeeping and reporting in *Danforth*. Thus, in order to ensure the constitutionality of zero tolerance drug policies, schools must provide a bypass option allowing violators to remain anonymous under certain circumstances.

When a school disciplines a student for violating its zero tolerance policy, the likelihood of the community discovering the minor's identity and the reason for the suspension is great. This likelihood creates an "unacceptable danger" of violating the minor's constitutional right of privacy when contraceptives are involved. The Supreme Court was unwilling to risk this danger when it dealt with abortion-reporting statutes, which provided less information about a woman's identity than is often obtained by a community regarding a minor who violates a zero tolerance policy. In addition, the Court has held that the protection from dissemination of one's private affairs is essential when the information at issue relates to the personal decision of whether to bear or beget a child. Furthermore, like the student's pregnancy at issue in *Gruenke*, a student's choice to use contraceptives is medical information protected from compelled disclosure by the Fourteenth Amendment. Accordingly, when a school disciplines a student under a zero tolerance drug policy for possessing contraceptives, the discipline often results in the reporting of the student's private affairs to the school community and to the public at large—a violation of the Fourteenth Amendment's informational privacy right.

Policies Are Too Broad

Zero tolerance advocates proffer several rationalizations for such policies, none of which justify infringement upon a minor's fundamental constitutional right of privacy. Proponents of zero tolerance have defended the policies by arguing that they protect students' health, keep schools safe, and have the general support of parents and school officials.

However, none of these rationalizations amount to a significant state interest not present in the case of an adult. First, the argument that regulations infringing upon the decision to use contraceptives are justified if they serve to protect health was rejected by the Supreme Court. While the desire to protect students allergic to certain medications is a laudable one, where such an attempt at protection sweeps up all prescription and over-the-counter medication in its path, including medical contraception, the policy is, like the statute at issue in *Eisenstadt*, overbroad and thus cannot justify the privacy infringement.

In addition, because the Court has held that a minor's privacy right outweighs the parental interest in notification, infringing upon a minor's contraceptive choices by enforcing zero tolerance drug policies cannot be justified simply by parental support for the policies. There is no significant state interest giving the state the constitutional authority to bestow a third party, parent or otherwise, with "an absolute, and possibly arbitrary, veto" over a minor's decision to exercise her constitutionally protected right. Further, "safeguarding of the family unit and of parental authority" is not a significant state interest sufficient to overcome a minor's privacy right. The same concerns in the abortion context that led the Court to require judicial bypass options make it evident that the arena of procreative-decision-making is one where a minor's interests at times trump those of the parents. Contraception is a topic on which "many parents hold strong views," and a minor's procreative decision-making should be based upon "the best interests of [the minor]." Thus, the concern that a parent or third party might exercise a "possibly arbitrary" veto over a minor's constitutionally protected private decision leads courts to invalidate parental consent requirements without judicial bypass options, putting the privacy interests of the minor before her parents' interests.

For the same reasons, a safety-based justification of zero tolerance policies must be rejected. A school could not constitutionally exercise what is effectively a third-party veto over a minor's procreative choices when the Court has held that the Constitution forecloses the minor's parents or other third party from doing just that. In addition, although the Court held in *Vernonia School District v. Acton* that infringement of student privacy rights may be justified by certain safety concerns related to drugs in schools, such policies are troublesome where they are conducted without confidentiality safeguards and they inquire into students' private medical affairs.

Schools Must Protect Students' Privacy

In sum, when a school district applies a zero tolerance policy to minors in possession of legally obtained contraceptives, the school cannot force a student to notify her parents of her procreative choices in order to comply with the policy. Such policies must include a bypass option that enables the student to avoid acquiring parental consent in order for the student to possess contraceptives at school. In addition, zero tolerance policies may not violate minors' constitutional right to be free from state dissemination of their private affairs—a natural consequence of disciplining students in possession of contraceptives in violation of the zero tolerance policy.

Schools violate their students' Fourteenth Amendment right of privacy when they apply zero tolerance drug policies to possession of medical contraceptives and require parental consent for a student to possess medical contraceptives and not run afoul of the policy. The constitutional right of privacy protecting an individual's procreative-related decision-making applies to minors as well as adults and does not disappear in the school setting. Unless a zero tolerance policy provides for an option (analogous to the "judicial bypass" of the abortion context) by which a student may avoid obtaining parental consent in order to "legally" possess medical contraceptives without first acquiring parental permission, the policy amounts to an unconstitutional mandatory parental consent requirement. In addition, a zero tolerance policy may not constitutionally compel a minor to notify a parent of the minor's private procreative decisions. Furthermore, because zero tolerance policies may not violate minors' constitutional right to be free from state dissemination of their private affairs, schools must take reasonable steps to insure that minors' procreative-related decisions will remain confidential.

NINE

Zero Tolerance Policies Treat Students as Criminals

Advancement Project

Advancement Project is a Washington, D.C.–based civil rights and legal advocacy group that works with communities across the United States to change racially discriminatory public policies. The following viewpoint argues that zero tolerance policies in schools often result in penalties that are out of proportion to student misbehavior. Numerous examples are given to show how school administrators and law enforcement agencies have overreacted to problems that previously would have been seen as harmless or careless mistakes made by children and teens. The long-term effects of zero tolerance policies on students who have been inappropriately disciplined are also discussed. The authors conclude that schools must re-examine zero tolerance policies and establish programs to teach appropriate behavior instead of only punishing misbehavior.

Across the United States many public schools have turned into feeder schools for the juvenile and criminal justice systems. Youths are finding themselves increasingly at risk of falling into the school-to-prison pipeline through push-outs (systematic exclusion through suspensions, expulsions, discouragement, and high-stakes testing). Yet, an even more direct schoolhouse-to-jailhouse track is transferring a growing number of youths to the penal system. In the name of school safety, schools have implemented unforgiving, overly harsh zero tolerance discipline practices that turn kids into criminals for acts that rarely constitute a crime when committed by an adult. No one is safe from zero tolerance—age, grade, past behavior, and disabilities are often irrelevant. And, although students of all races and genders are victims of this track, it is especially reserved for children of color—and males in particular. Schools have teamed up with law enforcement to make this happen by imposing a "double dose" of punishment: suspension or expulsion and a trip to the juvenile justice system.

At age 10, Porsche tragically became a passenger on the schoolhouse-to-jailhouse track. In December 2004, Porsche, a fourth-grade student at a Philadelphia, Pennsylvania, elementary school, was yanked out of class, handcuffed, taken to the police station and held for eight hours for bringing a pair of 8-inch scissors to school. She had been using the scissors to work on a school project at home. School district officials acknowledged that the young girl was not using the scissors as a weapon or threatening anyone with them, but scissors qualified as a potential weapon under state law.

"My daughter cried and cried," said Rose Jackson, Porsche's mother. "She had no idea what she did was wrong. I think that was way too harsh." Ultimately, city police did not charge Porsche with a crime because she had no intent to use the scissors as a weapon. She was, however, suspended from school for five days. School district officials later apologized, calling the school's actions extreme: "We do not think it's valid to call police officers off their beats to deal with nonthreatening incidents on a primary grade level. The school can handle these incidents using trained school police, our suspension and expulsion policies, and our mandated reporting as part of our zero tolerance policy."

A Drastic Response to Harmless Behavior

To some, American children have become Public Enemy #1. Society is becoming convinced that children are more violent than ever. Heavy media coverage of the rare instances of school violence has played into the public's worst fears and prompted a law-and-order approach to dealing with children. The truth is that between 1992 and 2002, nationwide violent crimes at schools against students aged 12 to 18 dropped by 50%, and schools remain the safest places for children. In addition, between 1994 and 2002, the youth arrest rate for violent crimes has declined 47% nationally.

Even in the face of these positive trends, schools are taking drastic steps. Visible measures to prevent serious crime in schools include: school security officers, police officers, metal detectors,

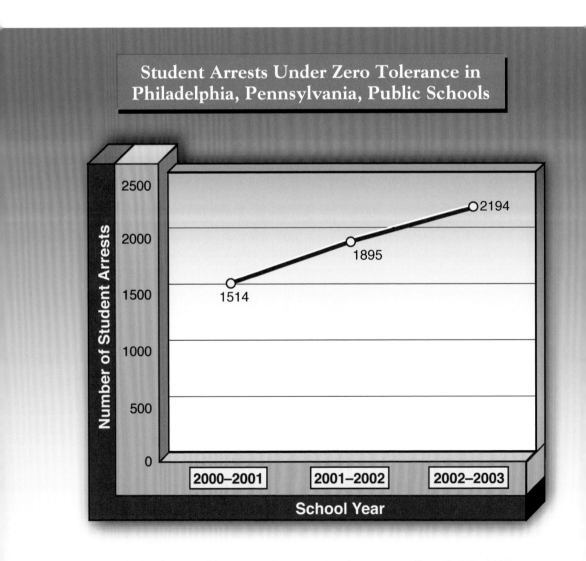

Student Arrests Under Zero Tolerance in Philadelphia, Pennsylvania, Public Schools

Taken from: Advancement Project, *Education Lockdown: The Schoolhouse to Jailhouse Track*, March 2005.

tasers, canine dogs, drug sweeps, SWAT teams, biometric hand readers, and surveillance cameras.

The untold story is the way in which schools are turning harmless acts of youthful indiscretion into crimes. In many instances zero tolerance policies have become ludicrous, and, even worse, are destroying thousands of children's lives by sending them into the juvenile justice system. Of course, we must have safety in our schools; however, a delicate balancing act must be applied. Schools must take a thoughtful approach to discipline to ensure that young men and women are not robbed of opportunities to succeed. . . .

The Long-Term Effects of Zero Tolerance

Zero tolerance has engendered a number of problems: denial of education through increased suspension and expulsion rates, referrals to inadequate alternative schools, lower test scores, higher dropout rates, and racial profiling of students. Also, according to the Center for Evaluation and Education Policy at Indiana University:

"Schools with higher rates of suspension have been reported to have higher student-teacher ratios and a lower level of academic quality, spend more time on discipline-related matters, pay significantly less attention to issues of school climate, and have less satisfactory school governance."

The criminalization of children by their schools leaves additional scars. These students face the emotional trauma, embarrassment, and stigma of being handcuffed and taken away from school—often shackled with an ankle-monitoring device. They must then serve time on probation with no slip-ups. One class missed or one filing grade and the next step may be a juvenile detention facility. Once many of these youths are in "the system," they never get back on the academic track. Sometimes, schools refuse to readmit them; and even if these students do return to school, they are often labeled and targeted for close monitoring by school staff and police. Consequently, many become demoralized, drop out, and fall deeper and deeper into the juvenile or criminal justice systems. Those who do not drop out may find that their discipline and juvenile or criminal records haunt them when they apply to college or for a scholarship or government grant, or try to enlist in the military or find employment. In some places, a criminal record may prevent them or their families from residing in publicly subsidized housing. In this era of zero tolerance, the consequences of child or adolescent behaviors may long outlive students' teenage years.

Zero Tolerance Penalties Are Inappropriate

In 2003, Advancement Project released its first comprehensive report on the criminalization of youths by their schools for minor conduct. *Derailed: The Schoolhouse to Jailhouse Track* detailed the growing expanse of zero tolerance policies and practices and the shift of school discipline for trivial incidents from principals' offices to police stations and courtrooms.

Since the publication of *Derailed*, a scan of news headlines reveals that the schoolhouse to jailhouse track is picking up steam. Some cases were so absurd, law enforcement or courts refused to deal with them. For example:

Monticello, FL—A 7-year-old, African-American boy who has Attention Deficit Disorder was arrested and hauled off to the county jail for hitting a classmate, a teacher, and a principal and scratching a school resource officer. The 4 foot, 6 inch, 60-pound second grader was fingerprinted and eventually cried himself to sleep in his jail cell.

Wilmington, NC—A high school student was criminally charged by a sheriff's deputy for cursing in front of a teacher. Four months after the student went to court, facing the possibility of up to 30 days in jail, prosecutors dropped the charges.

Bridgeport, CT—A high school student was arrested and charged with second degree breach of peace for a shouting argument with his girlfriend. Bridgeport students and parents protested the overreliance on law enforcement in schools after 140 students were arrested during the first six weeks of the school year.

Craig, CO—A 12-year-old student was charged with disorderly conduct for a shoving match with his classmate.

Port St. Lucie, FL—A 14-year old girl was arrested and charged with battery for pouring a carton of chocolate milk on the head

Students are often exposed to local law enforcement as a result of zero tolerance policies, which some feel has detrimental effects.

of a classmate. The girl explained that she heard that the victim was "talking about her." Local police stated that they believed "the quickest way to resolve it was to charge her."

Louisville, KY—An 8-year-old elementary school student was charged with felony assault when he hit and kicked his teacher as she attempted to remove him from the classroom for misbehaving. The juvenile court judge dismissed the charges.

These examples underscore the need to further examine the roles that schools and law enforcement play in needlessly criminalizing students and the consequences of that criminalization. . . .

Schools have turned to law enforcement to assist in school disciplinary matters. In many instances the conduct at issue is so petty, law enforcement agencies and courts have refused to pursue the charges that schools have initiated, which has had costly financial and human consequences. Ultimately, communities, parents, and students must hold school and law enforcement officials accountable for these actions, and urge them to create programs and practices that will teach appropriate behavior and not merely punish misbehavior.

Furthermore, schools must work toward creating environments that are safe and conducive to learning, but also where no youth is discarded or pushed out. Zero tolerance and the criminal treatment of students must not undermine the trust students place in their schools or cut off the bright futures of thousands of youths while adding nothing to the creation of safer learning environments.

TEN

Zero Tolerance Policies Target Minority Students

Annette Fuentes

> Annette Fuentes is an independent journalist and frequent contributor to the weekly political magazine *Nation*. In the following viewpoint, Fuentes argues that the implementation of zero tolerance policies has affected minority students far more seriously than white students. She outlines the history and development of zero tolerance policies in schools and explains how these policies have singled out minority students as juvenile delinquents. The result of this discrimination is that African American and Latino students are more likely to be funneled into the juvenile criminal justice system, which prevents them from receiving an adequate education. Fuentes concludes her argument with a summary of opinions from experts who agree that zero tolerance policies in schools ultimately cause more harm than good, particularly for minority students.

Bryson Donaldson, 12, was horsing around at his Muskogee, Oklahoma, school one morning . . . , mimicking the cops-and-robbers scenario that is as American as apple pie and Al Pacino. Bryson pointed his finger like a gun at a classmate and in a flash was hit with a five-day suspension. The principal singled out Bryson, the only African-American in his grade, for punishment, patting him down and scanning his sixth-grader's frame with a metal detector. He was placed in an alternative program for "bad" students, serving two days of his sentence until his mother brought in the NAACP [National Association for the Advancement of Colored People]. Bryson had been a straight-A student, but that changed. "He has nightmares now," Diane Donaldson said last June. "I had to take him to a psychiatrist. It is to the point where we have to struggle to go to school every day."

Some regard zero tolerance policies as harmful to minority students.

Daniel Brion, 14, was an eighth grader with a bright mind, a diagnosis of ADHD (attention deficit hyperactivity disorder) and a typical adolescent's jubilation as summer approached. . . . Walking down the hall of his Lexington, Kentucky, school, Daniel remarked that he wished the school would burn down and take the principal with it. His words were overheard and translated to said principal thusly: Daniel had gasoline and was recruiting a gang to burn down the school. Without notifying Daniel or his parents, the principal brought in the police to investigate Daniel's comments. Two weeks later, Daniel was yanked out of math class and interrogated by an officer who read him his Miranda rights. "The whole thing is like Franz Kafka's *The Trial*," said Dr. Gail Brion, his mother. "They were ready to arrest him on charges of terrorist threats."

The Unintended Results of Zero Tolerance

Every year, more than 3 million students like Bryson Donaldson are suspended and nearly 100,000 more are expelled, from kindergarten through twelfth grade. Of those, untold thousands like Daniel Brion increasingly face police action for disciplinary problem that were previously handled in school, because forty-one states now require that certain acts committed in school be reported to the police. Boys in general are the targets, with African-American males bearing a disproportionate brunt of suspensions and disciplinary actions. Together, these trends are the poisonous byproduct of a decade of so-called zero tolerance policies in public schools, from urban enclaves to rural outposts alike.

Youth advocates and education experts are increasingly alarmed about the toll of zero tolerance policies. While school administrators may believe suspensions and get-tough policies make schools safe and improve student behavior, the research shows otherwise. Excluding kids from school for two days or two months increases the odds of academic failure and dropping out. What's more, suspensions and academic failure are strong predictors of entry into the criminal justice system, especially for African-American males. That's why legal and education experts are blaming zero tolerance for what they call the "school to prison pipeline." If yesteryear's prank got a slap on the wrist, today those wrists could be slapped with handcuffs. "We are breeding a generation of children who think they are criminals for the way they are being treated in school," said Judith Browne, senior attorney at the Advancement Project, in Washington, DC. "School used to be a refuge. Now it's a lockdown environment. We are bringing the practices of criminal justice into the schools."

The Growth of Zero Tolerance in Schools

Zero tolerance was born during [former U.S. president Ronald] Reagan Administration's war on drugs, back in the mid-1980s. But it was [former U.S. president] Bill Clinton who gave it new currency in the schools when he signed the Gun-Free Schools Act of 1994, mandating expulsion of students who bring weapons to school. It was a time of public hysteria about youth crime, hyped by pop criminologists like James Q. Wilson, who predicted a violent juvenile crime wave, and John Dilulio, who coined the term "superpredator" to describe a new, vicious young criminal—the face of whom was implicitly a black or Latino urban male.

Racial coding and stereotypes infused such theories and fed the public's rampant fear of young minority males. The real dimensions of juvenile crime were far milder: a spike in violent crime that began in the late 1980s, crested in the early 1990s and has been falling ever since. At the time of the infamous 1999 Columbine [Colorado] High School shootings, incidents of school violence, including homicides, were at their lowest point in a decade. But by then, fear of African-American and Latino "ghetto gangstas" had expanded to include youth of all demographics, whether they lived in affluent white suburbs or poor black cities. Columbine only accelerated the zero tolerance juggernaut already in motion.

In the . . . years since then, states and localities have enacted policies in public schools that make the federal mandates look tepid. Broadened definitions of weapons and threatening behavior can turn a spitball into a deadly missile and a playground pushing match into an assault. What's more, zero tolerance is getting a boost from President [George W.] Bush's No Child Left Behind Act of 2001 and its focus on standardized-testing-as-educational-reform. "The wave of school shootings fed [the public's] concerns and states went wild with zero tolerance, giving principals total discretion to kick out any student they wanted," said Mark Soler, president of the Youth Law Center. "Now zero tolerance is fed less by fear of crime and more by high-stakes testing. Principals want to get rid of kids they perceive as trouble."

Students of Color Suffer from Over Zealous Discipline Policies

This chart compares the likelihood of student arrests by race or ethnicity.

White students

Latino and Native American students are 2.5 times as likely to be arrested as white students.

African American students are 5 times as likely to be arrested as white students.

Taken from: Sharon Smith, "Zero Tolerance Means Jail for Minority Youth," SocialistWorker.org, April 20, 2007.

Daniel Brion's school is typical in Kentucky, where zero tolerance took hold after a few incidents of school violence in the late 1990s, like the 1997 fatal shooting at a West Paducah high school prayer group. Yet school crime is very low in Kentucky, says Soler. For each of the past three years, for example, fewer than forty firearms offenses were reported for a student population of 625,000. But suspensions have multiplied: 65,508 in the 1999–2000 school year, and 68,523 the following year. Many of these were for "defiance of authority," a vaguely defined violation of school rules that was reported more than 25,000 times in the 2000–01 school year. "Defiance of authority is talking in class, talking back to teachers; it's irritating behavior. You can't have kids disturbing class, but schools have abdicated responsibility for finding a middle ground," said Soler. "The Kentucky data is clear. If you stop suspensions for minor behaviors, it would reduce the total number dramatically."

Zero Tolerance and Racial Profiling

Zero tolerance cheerleaders cite high rates of suspension and expulsion as the reason school violence is low. But no research supports that claim or the theory that zero tolerance improves academic outcomes. If anything, zero tolerance breeds failure among the most vulnerable students and puts kids on a path to prison, according to Russell Skiba, associate professor of education and director of the Safe and Responsive Schools Project at Indiana University. "Students suspended in elementary school are more likely to act out in middle school, and there is some correlation with dropouts. If one of the potent predictors of achievement is time spent learning, then expulsion's effect on achievement is not surprising," said Skiba. "Even if we say these are bad kids, zero tolerance doesn't do anything to help them. It's placing a higher proportion of students at risk for jail."

Skiba looked at zero tolerance policies in thirty-seven states using data from 2000 to gauge their relationship to achievement, behavior and youth incarceration. Schools with high out-of-school suspension rates had lower achievement in eighth-grade math, writing and reading. And states with higher school suspension rates were also more likely to have higher juvenile incarceration rates. Perhaps most sobering was the racial disparity: In almost every state, suspension, expulsion and incarceration rates were higher for African-Americans than for the general student population. In Minnesota 6 percent of all students were suspended in the 2000–01 school year, while 34 percent of African-American students were. African-American youth were more likely to be suspended and incarcerated than white children across the country, with many states guilty of staggering disproportion.

Southern states tend to have the highest absolute rates of suspension and juvenile incarceration, Skiba found, but the racial disparity is highest in the Midwest. In Minnesota, for example, African-American youth are nine times as likely to be suspended from school as white children and nine times as likely to be in jail. Skiba attributes the regional differences to the demographics and teacher quality of Midwestern urban areas, where African-Americans are concentrated. But the overall pattern of racial differences in school exclusion is another matter. "I'm beginning to think of this as an unplanned conspiracy," Skiba said. "When there is racial disparity, it reflects institutional behaviors perpetuated over time." National statistics on suspensions from the US Education Department for 2000 indicate the depth of the disparity: African-American students are 17 percent of the entire public school population but account for 34 percent of all out-of-school suspensions and 30 percent of expulsions. White students, by contrast, are 62 percent of the student population but account for 48 percent of out-of-school suspensions and 49 percent of expulsions.

African-American males face a double jeopardy with zero tolerance policies because they are often overrepresented in special education classes, where the federal Individuals with Disabilities Education Act doesn't always protect them from punitive discipline, according to Linda Raffaele Mendez, an associate professor in the department of school psychology at the University of South Florida. She looked at a thirteen-year study of schoolkids in Pinellas County, Florida, and found deep racial disparities in how suspensions were meted out. During their sixth-grade year, more than 66 percent of poor, black males with disabilities were suspended once, and many were suspended multiple times. "Special ed classes aren't much smaller, and teachers are often on emergency certification. They aren't prepared to work with these kids," Mendez said. "The zeitgeist [moral climate] now is zero tolerance, and that says you get the kid out when there is an infraction." Like Skiba, Mendez found a connection between suspensions and dropouts for all students. In the Pinellas cohort, a third of students disappeared between ninth and twelfth grades. "Kids are on a path. If they are suspended frequently at the end of elementary school, it's likely that will continue in middle school. And when they get to high school, it's very likely they will drop out," Mendez said.

Treating Students as Criminals

The school-to-prison pipeline often starts because teachers and principals are calling 911 and criminalizing student behaviors that in more tolerant times they would have handled themselves. "We're seeing very minor conduct becoming a criminal act. Things a police officer might not arrest someone for in a bar fight, we're seeing schools calling in police to make arrests for," said the Advancement Project's Browne.

Browne studied zero tolerance policies in Miami-Dade [Florida]. Palm Beach [Florida], Houston [Texas] and Baltimore [Maryland] schools, and found many arrests for disorderly conduct. "It could be a student who refuses to sit down in class, or the spitball," she said. "In addition to getting the three-to-five-day suspension, these kids are getting arrested." Browne said there are no statistics on the arrest trend nationally, and many districts don't keep data. But in Miami-Dade, Florida's largest district, arrests at school nearly tripled between 1999 and 2001, from 820 to 2,435 arrests. Of those, 28 percent were for "miscellaneous" offenses, and 29 percent were for simple assaults.

Texas schools have also elevated the trivial transgression to criminal levels. Students can be suspended and placed in an alternative program for cheating, violating dress codes, horseplay, excessive noise and failure to bring homework to class. When students are removed from school, it must be reported to the county juvenile justice board. That surprised Augustina Reyes, associate professor of education at the University of Houston and a former Houston school board member. "I knew there were a few alternative programs for difficult students, but I'd never seen the school disciplinary system become part of the juvenile justice system," said Reyes. "It concerned me that a 14-year-old could be removed from school and all of a sudden, he has a criminal record."

Reyes looked at statewide data on disciplinary actions for 2000–01 and found that almost half a million children from kindergarten through twelfth grade had been suspended from their classes, with a total of 1.1 million suspensions. What shocked her most, though, was the nature of school discipline: Of the total 1.7 million disciplinary actions that year, 95 percent were for discretionary reasons. "I thought I was going blind with the numbers," Reyes said. "When you see that only 5 percent of all kids are reported for mandatory reasons—cigarette smoking is a mandatory reason—I couldn't believe it."

Losing a Generation

Zero tolerance critics believe the current emphasis on standardized testing is one reason harsh policies continue even as school crime plummets. Central to No Child Left Behind are state and local mandates for annual testing of students in reading and math, and sanctions for those schools that fail to increase achievement. Reyes says the fixation on testing and a growing population of lower-income, mostly Latino, children in Texas public schools are incentives for suspension and exclusion. "I've seen how life on campus revolves around testing. If teachers are told, 'Your scores go down, you lose your job,' all of a sudden your values shift very quickly," she said. "Teachers think, 'With bad kids in my class, I'll have lower achievements on my tests, so I'll use discretion and remove that kid.'"

Judith Browne would like to see longitudinal studies on the relationship between high-stakes testing and the school-to-prison pipeline. "It makes sense that kids who don't pass these tests are being punished by being retained in a grade and are more likely to drop out and more likely to enter the criminal justice system," she said. Politically, zero tolerance reflects a steady and purposeful divestment in the public education system, and No Child Left Behind continues that political agenda with its underfunded and punitive mandates, according to Browne. "If we're right about what No Child Left Behind means, it is really a call for vouchers," she said. "It means, 'Let's set our schools up to fail so we can go to vouchers,' and there is language that allows transfers for schools that fail or are persistently violent, and each state can define what that means."

For Mark Soler, the fallout from zero tolerance policies extends far beyond the schoolhouse walls. "The great tragedy is, we're looking at losing an entire generation of children, particularly African-American," Soler said. "If we're going to kick kids out of school and put them on the pathway to prison, we'll end up with a whole generation of African-American men who cannot support themselves by lawful means and are less likely to be present husbands and fathers. The consequences for our communities are horrible."

ELEVEN

Zero Tolerance Policies Harm Teachers

Ron Isaac

Ron Isaac is a columnist for EdNews.org, an online clear-inghouse of education news and commentary. In the fol-lowing viewpoint, Isaac profiles a teacher who was sus-pended from work for violation of a school zero tolerance policy. Isaac describes the circumstances of the teacher's suspension, the immediate penalties, and the long-term effects on the teacher's career. Isaac shows the unfairness of the disciplinary action taken against the teacher, and expresses concerns that the quality of education will begin to suffer as teachers fear the consequences of potential zero tolerance policy violations.

These are stormy times for Dr. Leonard Brown, who is the classroom equivalent of a highly decorated field soldier. The dark skies opened up for him and the heavy rains starting falling [in November 2006] when he was pulled from Benjamin Cardozo High School in Queens [New York] and socked away in a Temporary Reassignment Center [TRC], better known by its gallows humor designation of "rubber room." He has been a physics instructor for eighteen years. Brown is no longer teach-ing Regents physics, chemistry, or mathematics. Today the only duty of this Ph.D. in Materials Science and Engineering, listed in

Who's Who Among America's Teachers, winner of the American Society for Metals Award for Excellence in Research, board member of numerous prestigious professional societies, and student-voted "Most Popular Science Teacher" is to clock in at the TRC. Why is that?

Dr. Brown has been charged with having made physical contact with a student because he asked her to hold her hands up against his and lean against his hands with all her weight: "Did you feel that?" Dr. Brown asked. "Feel what?" the student replied "Well, you're pushing against me with a force. Did you feel any opposition to that force?" "I think so." "How is that possible? After all, I wasn't pushing back on you. Or was I?" Why did Brown do this? He did this because he was demonstrating to 34 students one of the fundamental axioms of the subject they were studying: Newton's Law of Motion, which states that for every action there is an equal and opposite reaction. "How can we teach 'forces' without giving students a chance to experience what a 'force' feels like?" he wonders. When teaching about electrical circuits, for example, Brown explained the properties of a circuit by having the students make a "human" circuit, changing their "resistance" by having the students move closer together, and then examining how the motion of an electron (the student) is affected by pushing the student through the circuit. And yes, Dr. Brown played the battery.

For a generation he's got the lesson across the same way, without a hitch, much less a catastrophe. He never changed his M.O. You don't fix what's not broken. Brown says that physics is an intimidating and dry subject for many students, and his hands-on and sometimes whimsical approach has been fruitful in raising both students' confidence and academic performance. But now this author of a 450-page book on "The Dielectric Behavior of Plasma-Sprayed Coatings," grant writer, and supervisor of Westinghouse Science Talent Search winners, languishes in the TRC and yearns to get back to his students. "I'm afraid for the day when teachers will be afraid to do or say anything in the classroom that might spur students to greater achievement and a true love of learning. Education will be no more inspiring a challenge than memorizing the penal code," says Brown.

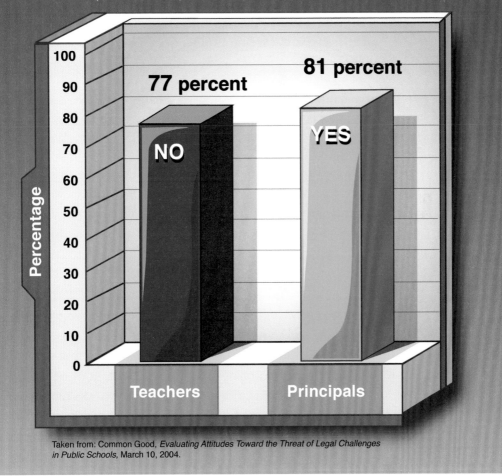

Teachers and Principals Respond

This graph shows the responses of teachers and principals to the question: "Do restrictive policies hurt your ability to do your job?"

77 percent

81 percent

NO

YES

Percentage

100
90
80
70
60
50
40
30
20
10
0

Teachers

Principals

Taken from: Common Good, *Evaluating Attitudes Toward the Threat of Legal Challenges in Public Schools*, March 10, 2004.

He demanded that he be given a lie detector test to help establish his right to return to the profession he loves. Although the test did not bear out the allegations, he has stayed put in a pernicious limbo:

Being denied the privilege to teach is almost as terrible as not being able to breathe. It took 2 months after I was sent away before I found out, through the rumor mill, the reason I was exiled. The respect for due process, which is becoming a rogue institution, is lost on the DOE [Department of Education]. The stakes are high. The road to justice should be clear, untainted, and unencumbered. A charade of justice is just another disguise for tyranny. How can there be a turf war between an employer and the United States Constitution?

Brown demands to know.

Removing Good Teachers from the Classroom

Irving Bass, who taught high school science for 52 years, says "I have had contact with literally hundreds of teachers, and Dr. Brown stands out as one of the best. He not only has a fantastic knowledge of physics, but he also has the unique ability to explain difficult concepts to his students. In addition to being an outstanding teacher, he has a genuine concern for his kids and a remarkable sense of humor. He is one of the rare and exceptional teachers who should be treasured. But sadly he has had to suffer the humiliation and indignity of being removed from his school and his students." Mr. Bass, whose last 40 years of teaching were at Cardozo High School and whose service at that school were still very much in demand until the day that Dr. Brown was removed, suddenly is no longer wanted there. He had expressed support for due process in the matter of Dr. Brown. According to Mr. Bass, that didn't sit well with the principal. "Due process is the core of our legal system and the cornerstone of the labor movement. I had to make my voice heard, no matter what. But I wish I didn't have to sacrifice my right to work in order to defend democracy," he says.

Dr. Brown says he will always love teaching, but is struggling against feeling jaded by the school system, and he . . . doesn't want it to be a losing battle for him as he has seen it to be for some others. "There are major abuses of power. Naturally there are some teachers who do not belong in a classroom. Of course we must keep predators away from children. But there's a huge difference between 'zero tolerance' and beyond zero tolerance." Sometimes where there's smoke there is no fire but conspiracy instead. Some of the DOE's targets are whistleblowers who had earlier exposed their current accusers. Others may have refused to knuckle under to irate or manipulative parents. Still others may have been the victim of kids who ganged up against them. It

Teachers in Austin, Texas, listen in on a news conference about legislation addressing teachers' use of discipline in the classroom.

may have been a spontaneous prank or a premeditated vendetta. Whether the intention was frivolous or malicious, the students may have been unaware of the consequences. Senior teachers may feel at enhanced risk because principals may want to rid their budgets of less cost-effective staff.

There are reportedly several other teachers from Cardozo who have been "removed" to TRCs also. The spike is mysterious. Brown feels that the truth would vindicate him, but tragically the DOE has no pure and genuine interest in discovering it. "They could care less about timeliness or burden of proof. They pick and choose witnesses with the same spirit as corrupt politicians who stuff ballot boxes. These unidentified witnesses can sink you but you can't cross examine them. Their statements often sound coached. There's got to be fairness and proportion. If a law is distorted and then used against you, it's just another kind of foul play. There is a witch hunt atmosphere."

A thick volume of letters of support keeps Brown company and brings him cheer as he fights for the truth to set him free. Here's one: "We are all pulling for you. You have a great weight on your shoulders. You did not deserve the treatment you received. It will take divine guidance to forgive those who made this happen." Now Brown faces charges against him pursuant to the 3020a State Education Law. It is widely perceived that the odds are stacked against teachers in these proceedings. If Brown does not prevail, he may lose his teaching license. The cost would be devastating to him, his family, his students, and do incalculable violence to the truth and the much cited honor of the law. If he were aggrieved by the outcome he could appeal to the Commissioner of Education. This can be a long and uncertain process and it is taking an astounding toll on a strong and good man. "All I want is to be reunited with my destiny: the joy of teaching children."

TWELVE

Zero Tolerance Policies Create Risks for Schools

Dave Lenkus

Dave Lenkus is a senior editor for *Business Insurance*. In the following viewpoint, Lenkus summarizes the need for risk management in school districts that maintain zero tolerance policies. Lenkus provides an overview of the risks and potential legal consequences of zero tolerance policies in schools. When zero tolerance policies are strictly implemented, the high risk of legal challenge can leave schools open to liability and lawsuits filed on behalf of students. The opinions of several experts are provided, along with recommendations for schools to protect themselves.

A kindergartener is arrested for violating her school's zero tolerance policy on weapons after she brings a pair of art scissors to class.

A third-grader is suspended for three months for violating her school's zero tolerance policy on drugs for bringing baby aspirin to school.

A high school student is suspended for violating his school's zero tolerance policy on fighting after a classmate with a history of behavioral problems sucker punches him and breaks his jaw.

The boy who assaulted his classmate never modifies his behavior despite all of the class time he missed throughout his school

Dustin Seal signs documents related to a settlement with the Knox County, Tennessee, school system. In 2001 Seal was paid $30,000 in the precedent-setting judgment over his expulsion from school in 1996, when a hunting knife was found in his car. His father has sued the school district for wrongful death after Dustin's 2002 suicide.

years due to numerous suspensions and expulsions. He was subsequently killed in a bar fight.

Those examples show the inadequacies of public schools' strict zero tolerance policies on potentially dangerous student behavior, according to school violence experts and national studies on school crime and childhood development. The anecdotes underscore that the policies—by themselves—are usually ineffective, often unfair, sometimes ludicrous and potentially harmful, experts say.

Risk Management in Schools

Ten years of school violence research shows that schools create safer cultures by implementing less rigid discipline policies that are underpinned by programs designed to prevent problematic student behavior, concluded the Zero Tolerance Task Force of the American Psychological Association in an August 2006 report. Other child and antiviolence experts concur.

Although they typically were not involved in developing the policies and have no official role in evaluating them, school district risk managers should insert themselves into the issue of school discipline and behavioral programs, several experts say. The safety and liability and even school culture issues that arise from ineffective discipline policies are clearly risk management concerns, they say.

Zero tolerance policies, introduced in the early 1990s to discourage drug abuse and later applied to numerous rules on student behavior, send a strong message that schools will deal sternly with students over any behavior that could harm others or themselves. Students who violate those policies—regardless of extenuating circumstances—typically face suspension and expulsion and oftentimes arrest.

The problem with those policies is that school officials typically use them as a quick solution to behavioral issues in place of the more painstaking approach of exercising good judgment on a case-by-case basis, experts say.

"More often than not, zero tolerance was first instituted because people didn't know how to respond to instances they could be flexible with," said Gary Salmans, a Troy, Michigan–based executive VP of risk management services in the Critical Incident Prevention Management division of Arthur J. Gallagher & Co.

The term zero tolerance "sounds real good," said school violence consultant David L. Salmon, a senior advisor with OSS Law Enforcement Advisors of Spring, Texas. "It has a political ring to it. It doesn't have a practical ring to it."

Some school districts are beginning to agree, though many school officials are reticent about discussing decisions to abandon or modify their long-standing policies and, instead, address student problems on a case-by-case basis, expert say. Still, many primary and secondary schools continue to enforce strict zero tolerance policies, according to experts.

According to the latest federal statistics, student safety nationwide has improved in nonfatal crimes, but the student homicide rate—while generally below the rate during the 1990s—has worsened this decade. Meanwhile, during the 2003–2004 school year, the nation's 36,800 public schools seriously disciplined 655,700 students, with suspensions of five days or longer accounting for 74% of those actions, according to government statistics. But removing disruptive students from the structured environment that schools provide often is ineffective and many times only worsens the problem, experts say.

Risk managers can and should play a role in helping to reform those policies, experts say. "I feel their input should be part of the process," said Katharine M. Peeling, the outgoing president of the Public Risk Management Association and risk management specialist in the Office of Insurance Management at Anne Arundel County Public Schools in Annapolis, Maryland. Ms. Peeling does not have formal responsibility for discipline procedures in her school district but has inserted herself into the process.

There are two major reasons why other risk managers need to get involved, she said. First, "when you have unreasonable policies, you're going to get sued," she said. "Risk managers would have a much better understanding of the fallout" of disciplinary programs that are ineffective, said Ms. Peeling, referring to, for example, continuing school violence and associated litigation.

Dorothy Gjerdrum, the St. Paul, Minnesota–based executive director of the public entity and scholastic division at Arthur J. Gallagher and Co., agreed on the need for risk management involvement. Any time there is "a break between policy and enactment of a policy, there's a potential for liability," she said. For schools, that risk is created when zero tolerance policies are implemented but school faculty and administrators are not trained in how to apply those policies appropriately, Ms. Gjerdrum said.

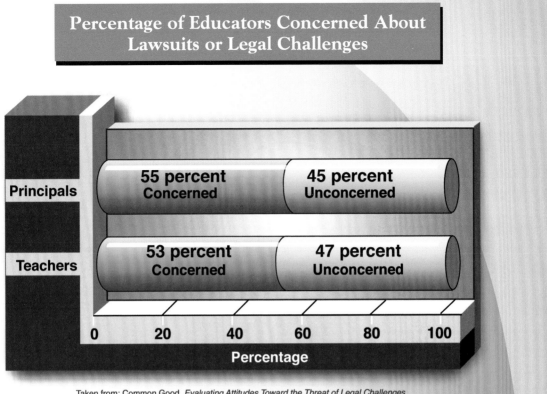

Percentage of Educators Concerned About Lawsuits or Legal Challenges

Principals
55 percent Concerned
45 percent Unconcerned

Teachers
53 percent Concerned
47 percent Unconcerned

0   20   40   60   80   100

Percentage

Taken from: Common Good, *Evaluating Attitudes Toward the Threat of Legal Challenges in Public Schools*, March 10, 2004.

Ms. Peeling and Ms. Gjerdrum also agreed that risk managers could and should play an important role in shaping school culture. Ms. Gjerdrum said that risk management input on matters that affect school culture would reflect an enterprise risk management perspective, "which is really starting to emerge" among other types of public entities. Regardless of a school district official's title or formal duties, "We're all here for the same thing—we're all here to educate the kids," Ms. Peeling said. For children to learn and achieve the level of test scores that a school desires, "there has to be a safe school environment."

School Liability

Some critics would like to see schools abandon zero tolerance policies. The idea is not to give up on holding dangerous or self-destructive students accountable for their actions but to give school officials and the police greater latitude in how they deal with incidents. For police in particular, zero tolerance policies can be problematic, said Mr. Salmon of OSS. When police follow those policies and arrest students for noncriminal school code infractions, they could lose their qualified immunity for failing to use discretion, which is a key issue in police immunity cases, he said.

But police often follow those policies because of a lack of adequate training in this area, said Mr. Salmon, who also is a police academy instructor. "It's very confusing to police." Meanwhile, such cases typically go nowhere because juvenile courts toss them out, he said. That can lead to one or two problems, he said: The school's authority is weakened in the eyes of its students, and the incidents sometimes promote harassment of the arrested student.

Experts noted that zero tolerance policies on bullying and fighting also often backfire. Experts say they often see schools mete out comparable discipline to both a bully and the student who fought back against a tormentor. "That's the best example of zero tolerance not working that I've ever seen," Mr. Salmon said.

Gallagher's Mr. Salmans also is critical of strict zero tolerance policies, but he said schools do not have to abandon them. A school still could enforce a zero tolerance policy against fighting, for example, he said. But the policy should spell out how an instigator would be treated differently from the other brawling student. To ensure that a disciplinary action is appropriate, a committee of school officials should evaluate each case, he said.

Ms. Gjerdrum, however, is not as critical of strict zero tolerance policies as she is of a lack of multi-pronged and coordinated programs to reduce risk stemming from student behavior. "It's sort of a tricky question," Ms. Gjerdrum said, "because it's not the policy itself that creates the risk; it's the lack of coordination or implementation of other important and related program and activities," such as staff and student training, safety and security and employee assistance programs for employees who feel stressed by the school environment.

How risk managers win a seat at the table where discipline policies and behavioral programs are formulated will vary depending on the school officials and risk managers involved, she said. "For administrators, it's very hard to respond to things before they happen," so risk managers would have to "use some of their softer skills" to play a role in their schools' zero tolerance policies, Ms. Gjerdrum said. Risk managers have to communicate to those responsible for the policies the threats that the policies can create, then offer to help minimize those risks, she said.

One way to step into the process is to find a high-ranking official to help champion the risk manager's effort, Ms. Gjerdrum said. Another approach would be to use professional associations to network with other risk managers who have addressed this issue, she said. Or, risk managers who already have substantial clout in their districts might consider forming a cross-discipline task force to examine the issue, Ms. Gjerdrum said.

All of those methods point to the underpinnings of effective risk management, Ms. Peeling said "You can't shove risk management down peoples' throats; it won't work," she said. "They have to think it's a good idea."

THIRTEEN

Zero Tolerance Policies Create Controversy

Russell Skiba et al.

Russell Skiba is a professor at Indiana University and Director of the Equity Project, a research consortium focusing on school discipline. He is also a past member of the American Psychological Association Task Force on Zero Tolerance. In the following viewpoint, Skiba questions the manner in which some schools are defining weapons, drugs, and misbehavior under zero tolerance. Skiba argues that zero tolerance policies are controversial in part because these definitions are too broad. Zero tolerance policies were originally intended to protect students and teachers from serious harm. He gives numerous examples of cases in which students were strictly disciplined for incidents that did not seem to pose any real threat to the safety of others. The confusing and contradictory use of zero tolerance policies in some schools has caused many people to question the validity of such policies.

From their inception in the 1980s, zero tolerance policies and practices have been consistently controversial. The harsh punishments meted out for relatively minor infractions in the early zero tolerance drug cases raised a host of civil rights concerns: The

American Civil Liberties Union considered filing suit on behalf of those whose automobiles, boats, and even bicycles had been impounded with trace amounts of marijuana (Hansen, 1988). By 1990, the Customs Service zero tolerance boat impoundment program was quietly phased out after a Woods Hole Oceanographic Institute research vessel was seized for a marijuana cigarette found in a seaman's cabin.

Similar controversy has attended a host of suspensions and expulsions associated with zero tolerance for relatively trivial incidents in school settings. Literally thousands of media reports since the late 1980s have brought individual zero tolerance school disciplinary incidents to the public attention. In the following sections, we examine a few of these incidents, organized by weapons, threats, drugs, and other:

Defining "Weapons"

The Gun-Free Schools Act [GFSA] bans the possession of a firearm on school grounds and mandates a one-year expulsion for that offense. Yet school districts have extended that policy considerably, with wide variation in what might be considered a weapon:

October, 1999, Atlanta, Georgia: A 15-year-old South Cobb High School sophomore found with an unloaded gun in his book bag was permanently expelled from the school district. "That is the standard we have set in the past for anyone that has brought a weapon to school," said the district's associate superintendent. "It's extremely serious, dangerous for everybody involved." The youth was also charged in juvenile court with possession of a weapon (Stepp, 1999).

March, 2002, Hurst, Texas: A bread knife was found in the back of a truck of a high school junior who had been helping his father take a load of possessions from his grandmother to Goodwill the previous weekend. The boy, an honors student and award-winning swimmer at the school, was expelled for one year to the Tarrant County Juvenile Justice Alternative Education Program. Said the boy's father, "It's crushing. That is for hard-core, violent youth" (Mendoza, 2002).

September, 2000, Atlanta, Georgia: An eleven-year-old girl was suspended for two weeks from Garrett Middle School for possession of a 10-inch novelty chain attaching her Tweety Bird wallet to her key ring. School officials stated that district policy was clear, classifying a chain as a weapon, in the same category as pellet guns, ice picks, and swords. The American Civil Liberties Union filed a lawsuit on behalf of the girl, noting that students had been previously suspended in the district for a plastic knife used to cut a cake, bracelets and necklaces, and a screwdriver used to fix a band instrument (Rodriguez, 2000).

November, 1997, Dublin, Ohio: A seventh-grade boy who brought in a toy cowboy gun for a skit in French class with the permission of the teacher was suspended for five days and received zeroes for all work during the period of the suspension. "For a skit on Old Yeller, I had brought in a much larger toy rifle," the boy noted. "I got extra credit" (Ellis, 2003).

These incidents highlight two sources of controversy created by zero tolerance incidents. In the Atlanta case involving a shotgun in a backpack, there can be little doubt of the seriousness of the offense; in this case however, it is not the necessity of the expulsion under the GFSA, but rather its length that makes the incident newsworthy. In other cases, controversy has been created by defining as a weapon an object, such as a chain attached to a Tweety Bird wallet, which poses little real danger. The unwillingness of many school districts involved in such incidents to back down suggests that the extension is intentional and consistent with the philosophical intent of zero tolerance, treating both major and minor incidents with severity in order to set an example to others. This stance appears to take some zero tolerance applications well beyond the statutory mandates of the Gun-Free Schools Act. That act states that an instrument that otherwise might be construed as a weapon will not trigger a mandatory expulsion if it is for "activities approved and authorized" by the local educational agency; one might presume that a cowboy gun brought to class for a skit in French class would constitute an activity approved and authorized by the local educational agency.

Evaluating Threats of Violence

Recent incidents of lethal school violence, and the copy-cat threats those incidents have occasionally spawned, have made school personnel especially sensitive to threats of violence in school. It is not surprising that zero tolerance has been a strategy chosen by some schools and districts to address real or perceived threats.

A student at Shaler Area High School in Pennsylania stands in the corner of Shaler District Justice Robert Dzvonick's office, as punishment for inappropriate behavior at school.

March, 2001, Topeka, Kansas: At Wabaunsee High School, a 15-year-old student wrote a message that he was going to "get you all" on the boys' bathroom wall. After the message was erased by the school, he wrote a second message stating that he should be taken seriously and was "going to shoot everyone." The boy, arrested and charged with one count of criminal threat, returned to school after a five-day suspension. Some parents protested the leniency of the school punishment. "I know kids who have been suspended for three days just for orneriness and this kid threatened to kill the whole student body," complained one parent (Grenz, 2001).

March, 2001, Irvington, New Jersey: Two second-graders were suspended and charged by local juvenile authorities with making terroristic threats after pointing a piece of paper folded to look like a gun at classmates and saying "I'm going to kill you all." The superintendent of the district noted that "I thought this was very unfortunate. But, being that kids are being shot in schools across the country, children have to be taught they can't say certain words in public." The father of one of the boys disagreed, however, stating, "This is just stupid, stupid, stupid. How can you take two boys to the police precinct over a paper gun? This is very bad judgment" (Associated Press, 2001).

April, 2001, Chicago, Illinois: After a band concert, a junior at suburban Reavis High School and three friends put together a list of twenty members of fellow band members they did not like. When rumors spread that the list was really a "hit list," the student, acknowledged as an active and bright student, was suspended for four days and excluded from band. "It's crazy," stated the boy's mother, herself an assistant principal at Chicago high school. "There's a difference between saying 'I'm going to come to school with a gun and blow everybody up,' and saying, 'Here are kids who annoy me'" (Sternberg, 2001).

Recent school shooting incidents provide an unequivocal lesson that schools must have policies and procedures in place to investigate and respond to threats, and may place themselves at risk by ignoring serious threats of violence. It is not surprising then, to see an increase in zero tolerance practices regarding threat in the aftermath of school shootings and copy-cat threats of school shootings. Indeed, some reactions to threat may be perceived by the community as too lenient, as in the case of the threat at Waubansee High School. Yet the local and in some cases national furor created by some of these incidents suggests

Educators and Parents Do Not Agree About the Effectiveness of School Discipline

Ninety percent of principals and 57 percent of teachers believe discipline in their school is fair.

Taken from: Common Good, "Evaluating Attitudes Toward the Threat of Legal Challenges in Public Schools," March 10, 2004.

Forty-three percent of parents believe their child's school could handle student misbehavior better.

Taken from: Public Agenda, "Teaching Interrupted: Do Discipline Policies in Today's Public Schools Foster the Common Good?" May 2004.

that there may be limits on what a school can or should do to protect staff and students. Indeed, automatic school exclusion for threats of violence is unlikely to solve the complex problems of threatened violence in schools. In its report *School Shootings: A Threat Assessment Perspective*, the FBI issued a strong caution:

> It is especially important that a school not deal with threats by simply kicking the problem out the door. Expelling or suspending a student for making a threat must not be a substitute for careful threat assessment and a considered, consistent policy of intervention. Disciplinary action alone, unaccompanied by any effort to evaluate the threat or the student's intent, may actually exacerbate the danger—for example if a student feels unfairly or arbitrarily treated and becomes even angrier and more bent on carrying out a violent act (O'Toole, 2000, p. 26).

Best practice in threat assessment recommends instead that schools conduct a comprehensive threat assessment to determine the seriousness of any threat, and develop a team approach to threat evaluation and intervention (Cornell & Sheras, 2006).

Alcohol and Drugs

Although there is no federal mandate of suspension or expulsion for drug-related offenses, the application of zero tolerance to drugs or alcohol has become quite common.

June, 1998, Brookline, Massachusetts: Nine seniors caught with alcohol on a bus going to their senior prom were barred by the principal from attending their graduation, and two were not allowed to compete in the state baseball playoffs. Citing tragic accidents caused by alcohol abuse, Brookline High School Headmaster Robert Weintraub stated, "Every time there's a serious incident, a violation of drugs, alcohol, or weapons, I have taken a very hard line, because it's important for kids to get the message that if they do something that violates some of the fundamental rules we have here, they will be punished" (Abrahms, 1998).

October, 1998, East Lake, Florida: High school senior Jennifer Coonce took a sip of sangria at a luncheon with co-workers as part of a school-sponsored internship. When her parents called the high school to complain about minors being served alcohol, the district suspended her for the remainder of the semester. Jennifer, an honors student, was offered the opportunity to take her college placement classes at home, over the telephone (Smith, 1998).

January, 2004, Bossier Parrish, Louisiana: A fifteen-year-old girl found in possession of one Advil tablet was expelled for one year under a district policy of zero tolerance for any drug. Closer scrutiny of previous school disciplinary actions in the school district revealed cases in which other students had received a lighter punishment for explicitly illegal drugs. As a result of local furor surrounding the case, Bossier Parrish school officials rewrote the policy to allow school principals to have greater discretion in determining which drugs would fall under the policy ("One headache cured," 2004).

The fact that a wide range of incidents are met with very similar punishment may shed light on why zero tolerance creates controversy. Stiff punishments for serious drinking or drug abuse at school-sponsored events seem appropriate and may well serve to prevent more serious harm. In contrast, removing a child from school for possession of an over-the-counter headache tablet or punishing relatively minor off-campus behavior seems more likely to turn the offender into the perceived victim. Strictures against cruel and unusual punishment are enshrined in our legal system and Bill of Rights: School punishments that appear to be greatly out of proportion to the offense may create controversy by violating basic perceptions of fairness inherent in our system of law, even when those punishments are upheld by the courts.

Disobedience and Misbehavior

Federal legislation in the Gun-Free Schools Act applies zero tolerance only to firearms on school grounds. Many school systems have extended the reach of zero tolerance policy to a range of behaviors or incidents that do not involve weapons and that do not necessarily threaten the safety of the school environment.

February, 2005, Adams City, Colorado: When 15 students who attended Adams City High School watched a fight between two students in a nearby park, the school principal made a recommendation that all 17 students be expelled for one year. The students were suspended for two months before the school board ordered that the students who had watched the fight be allowed to return to school (Poppen, 2005).

May, 2005, Highlands Ranch, Colorado: An 11-year-old at Cresthill Middle School who took a lollipop from a jar on the teacher's desk was charged with theft after charges were filed by the classroom teacher and the school principal. The boy, who claimed he did not know the candy was being sold to raise money, was convicted of a misdemeanor and is currently on probation (Rodriguez, 2005).

May, 2005, Columbus, Georgia: A junior at Spencer High School in Columbus, Georgia, was suspended for 10 days for violation of district cell phone policy when he refused to hand over his cell phone to a teacher while talking [to] his mother serving in Iraq for the first time in a month. Although the boy stated he did not lose his temper and was "simply being insistent" about talking to his mother, school officials said he was being "very defiant" and that this was "not an isolated incident with this particular student." The boy's guardian, Staff Sgt. Shalita Hartwell, said, "I'm perturbed and his mom is perturbed. Anyone would have an attitude if they snatched the phone away when talking to his mother" (Torpy, 2005).

As in other categories, the apparent degree of threat posed by the infraction to school safety varies in these incidents. Although the first incident may have involved suspected gang members, the latter two incidents involve extensions of zero tolerance that appear to be issues of school policy more than school safety. The second incident is noteworthy as an example of the increasing willingness among some administrators to use juvenile justice consequences for school-related behavior (Casella, 2003). Finally, it is noteworthy that one administrative justification for the cell phone incident described above was a previous disciplinary action involving the boy. While it is common for school administrators to take previous disciplinary history into account in assigning school punishments, the use of that type of contextual information appears to contradict the assumption that zero tolerance punishments are certain, invariant, and context-free.

References

Abrahms, S. (1998, June 21). Discipline of 9 seniors is evaluated: Headmaster defends 'zero tolerance' stance. *Boston Globe*, p. 1.

Associated Press. (2001, March 22). Second-graders facing charges. *Newsday*, p. A33.

Casella, R. (2003). Zero tolerance policy in schools: Rationale, consequences, and alternatives. *Teachers College Record, 105*, 872–892.

Cornell, D. G., & Sheras P. L. (2006). *Guidelines for responding to student threats of violence*. Boston: Sopris West Educational Services.

Ellis, M. (2003, November 28) Student recalls strife caused by toy pistol. *Columbus Dispatch*, p. 01F.

Grenz, C. (2001, March 31). Accused student to return to class. *Topeka Capital-Journal*.

Hansen, M. (1988, June 22). ACLU studies fight of zero tolerance. *Los Angeles Times*, p. B3.

Mendoza, M. (2002, March 19). Honor student expelled over bread knife in truck. *Fort Worth Star-Telegram*, p. A20.

O'Toole, M.E., & the Critical Incident Response Group (2000). *The school shooter: A threat assessment perspective*. Quantico, VA: Federal Bureau of Investigation. http://www.fbi.gov/library/school/school2.pdf.

One headache cured. (2004, January 13). *Times-Picayune* (New Orleans, LA), p. 4.

Poppen, J. (2005, April 1). Adams City High suspensions may violate policy. *Rocky Mountain News* (Denver, CO), p. 26A.

Rodriguez, C. (2005, April 5). $1 candy theft a misdemeanor? *Denver Post*, p. F-01.

Rodriguez, Y. (2000, September 28). Cobb school calls wallet chain a weapon, suspends girl, 11. *Atlanta Journal-Constitution*, p. 1A.

Smith, A. C. (1998, November 14). Court casts doubt on 'zero tolerance' policy. *St. Petersburg Times*, p. 1B.

Stepp, D. R. (1999, October 12). Cobb expels student for packing gun. *Atlanta Journal-Constitution*, p. 3C.

Sternberg, N. (2001, April 6). Paranoid times chill fair play. *Chicago Sun-Times*, p. 3.

Torpy, B. (2005, May 7). Teen punished for taking Iraq cell call; Chat with Army mom violated school policy. *Atlanta Journal-Constitution*, p. 1A.

FOURTEEN

Zero Tolerance Policies Are Losing Support from Schools and Government

Kavan Peterson

Kavan Peterson is a staff writer for Stateline.org, a daily online publication of the Pew Research Center, which studies social and state-government policy. In the following report, Peterson describes some of the unintended consequences of zero tolerance policies and the resulting debate over the balance between safety and tolerance in schools. Cases in which students' punishment seemed unnecessarily harsh have focused public attention on the ways in which zero tolerance policies are not working. Peterson discusses the backlash against zero tolerance policies in schools, including legislation in several states that would eliminate the policies.

When schools began greatly expanding zero-tolerance policies against student misbehavior after the shootings at Columbine [Colorado] High School in 1999, few expected to see kids as young as 6 handcuffed and removed from school for throwing a temper tantrum or playing with squirt guns. With nearly half of states now mandating that schools expel and often call the police on students for fighting, possessing weapons of any kind or even disrupting class, thousands of students nationwide have been kicked out of school or seen the inside of a cop car for violating zero-tolerance policies.

Kavan Peterson, "Schools Rethink Post-Columbine Discipline," Stateline.org, March 14, 2005. Reproduced by permission of Stateline.org.

Now, recent outcries over arrests of elementary students and mounting evidence that zero-tolerance policies adversely impact disadvantaged students have sparked a debate over the proper balance between safety and tolerance in America's schools. Some of the first stirrings of a possible retrenchment can be seen in three states—Indiana, Mississippi and Texas—where a handful of lawmakers are trying to reverse the trend of adopting ever-more stringent discipline policies.

Highly publicized arrests in Florida and Nevada in the past two months [2005] are among dozens of examples where zero-tolerance policies have gone too far, critics say. In January, two grade-school children were arrested in Ocala, Florida, for drawing threatening stick figures in class. A 6-year-old in Florida's Brevard County was handcuffed and removed from school for hitting his teacher and a police officer with a book. And in Nevada, Clark County School District officials recently tried to expel a student who drew a comic strip depicting the death of his teacher. "Clearly I think there are incidents that are so excessive that the facts show that this is a mindless policy in most places," said Mark Soler, president of the Youth Law Center, a Washington, D.C.–based law firm that works on child-welfare and juvenile justice system issues.

Some school officials and police say parents concerned about safety have demanded such stepped-up vigilance and discipline, and leave them no alternative but to have children removed from school and sometimes entered into the criminal justice system. To critics, however, there is scant evidence that zero-tolerance policies increase school safety and mounting evidence that harsh discipline may do more harm than good. "There is no data that zero tolerance makes a difference either in improving school climate or improving student behavior," said Russ Skiba, an education psychology professor at Indiana University and the director of the Center for Evaluation and Education Policy.

In fact, the data point the other direction, said Skiba, who has done several studies critical of zero-tolerance policies. "There's abundant evidence that suspensions/expulsions disproportionately fall upon minority students, and there are direct correla-

Percentage of West Virginia residents who agree that public school classroom discipline needs to be improved:

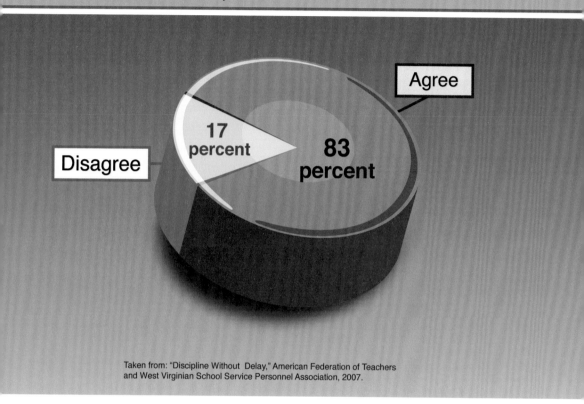

17 percent

83 percent

Disagree

Agree

Taken from: "Discipline Without Delay," American Federation of Teachers and West Virginian School Service Personnel Association, 2007.

tions between use of suspensions/expulsions to dropout rates and juvenile incarceration," he said. In a study released in summer 2004, Skiba reported that African-American students in Indiana are four times more likely to get suspended and two-and-a-half times more likely to be expelled than white students. Previous studies have found no evidence that this is due to higher rates of misbehavior by minority students, Skiba said. Instead, African-American and Hispanic students appear to be suspended and expelled for more subjective and minor infractions than white students, he said.

Backers of zero-tolerance policies say that tactics such as installing metal detectors, creating crisis-response plans and cracking down on bullying, unruly and suspicious behavior have led to a dramatic drop in school-related violence. They point to a federal report issued in December 2004 that showed violent crime in schools fell 50 percent between 1992 and 2002, a striking decline that mirrors the national drop in crime. The U.S. Centers for Disease Control and Prevention also found a drop in the number of weapons students admitted bringing to school in a national survey. The center reported that 6.1 percent of high school students admitted they had carried a gun, knife, or club on school property in 2003, down from 6.9 percent in 1999.

The Columbine school shooting in Colorado—in which Dylan Klebold and Eric Harris killed 12 students and a teacher before committing suicide—was the worst in a series of a dozen school shootings in the United States over an 18-month period. Although children actually are much safer in school than out— the chance of becoming a victim in a school-associated violent death is less than one in a million, according to the Youth Law Center—these incidents had an enormous effect on public perceptions of school danger.

Zero-tolerance policies were not new in 1999, but in the wake of Columbine, they were dramatically expanded by state legislatures and school districts to include not just weapons and drugs, but fighting and misbehavior. Now the list of infractions that can get students expelled or arrested tops 20, ranging from swearing and insubordination to making terrorist threats or skipping school. Under federal law, all states must adopt zero-tolerance policies for firearms. But since Columbine, zero-tolerance policies have been adopted for fighting in 23 states, for disrupting class in 19 states, and kids can be expelled for making threats in 12 states, according to the Center for Evaluation and Education Policy.

The tide may be turning, however. Few states have recently expanded their zero-tolerance policies, and [in 2005], several lawmakers introduced bills to roll them back. In Texas, zero-tolerance policies have resulted in a disproportionate number of low-income, disabled and minority students being sent to alternative disciplinary schools, most of which have few books or computers and substandard teachers, said Texas state Rep. Dora Olivo, a Democrat. "What makes me really concerned is that the majority of kids sent to disciplinary schools are poor kids, almost all black and brown children," Olivo said. Olivo introduced a bill that would make

While addressing the annual convention of the National Education Association in 1996, then-President Bill Clinton urged zero tolerance for truancy. Since then, government support for zero tolerance policies has eroded.

schools responsible for the assessment test scores of students who are transferred into disciplinary schools. Olivo said there is an incentive for school officials to warehouse low-achieving students in disciplinary schools in an attempt to raise their school's overall test scores. The measure passed the Texas House in March 2005 and [was] considered by the Senate.

The national movement toward school accountability and mandatory testing, such as President [George W.] Bush's sweeping No Child Left Behind law, which penalizes schools that do not raise student test scores, has lead to abuse of zero-tolerance policies, said Soler of the Youth Law Center. Increasingly, he said, groups who perform poorly on standardized tests, such as students with disabilities, minorities and low-income kids, are targeted for expulsion by school administrators and kicked out for minor infractions. "It's a real problem because raising test scores is becoming a major part of (employment) contracts for principals and school administrators, and they are ready to do anything to make sure that their schools look good," Soler said.

Another bill pending in Texas, introduced by Republican state Sen. Jon Lindsay, would require that a student's intent be considered in reaction to any incident. In Mississippi, Democratic state Rep. Eric Fleming introduced a bill that would prohibit schools from zero-tolerance policies. And legislation has been introduced in Indiana to study why African-American and Hispanic students are suspended more frequently than white students.

What You Should Know About Zero Tolerance Policies in Schools

What Is a Zero Tolerance Policy?

A zero tolerance policy is a rule or law that completely forbids certain behavior and requires punishment for all violations, regardless of individual circumstances or explanation. Zero tolerance policies use the threat of severe consequences to discourage behavior that is deemed aggressive, destructive, unsafe, illegal, and/or unethical. The goal of a zero tolerance policy is to eliminate behaviors that are harmful or potentially harmful.

Who Uses Zero Tolerance Policies?

Elementary, middle, and high schools are not the only places where zero tolerance policies are used. Strict disciplinary policies, with zero tolerance for violations, are often used by employers, government, law enforcement agencies, the military, universities, and other organizations. Many of these zero tolerance policies focus on activities that are against the law, such as the use of illegal drugs, possession of an unregistered or stolen gun, drunk driving, stealing, injuring or attacking another person, and so on. One example of a nationwide zero tolerance policy is the list of items that passengers are forbidden to bring on an airplane.

Some of these zero tolerance policies also cover activities that may not be illegal, but that are deemed inappropriate or potentially harmful, such as cheating on a test, lying about previous work experience or education, drinking alcohol while at work, or not showing up for work at all. Many professional organizations, such as those that issue licenses to doctors and lawyers, have strict disciplinary policies for any violation of professional ethics or code of conduct.

Schools and Zero Tolerance Policies

Zero tolerance policies became common in American elementary, middle, and high schools during the mid-1990s. The federal Gun-Free Schools Act of 1994 requires school districts to have zero tolerance policies for guns in order to continue receiving government funding for school programs. This law requires schools to implement specific punishments for any student who brings a gun to school, including a one-year expulsion and the mandatory involvement of the local police department.

Concerns about school safety have grown as a result of tragic incidents of violence in schools across the country. In response, some states and local school districts have used the requirements of the Gun-Free Schools Act as a starting point for zero tolerance policies, adding a range of offenses that do not necessarily involve guns. While each school or district zero tolerance policy may be unique, these expanded policies commonly forbid students to:

- Bring a weapon of any kind to school or a school event
- Sell or give a weapon to another student
- Possess any type of explosive
- Provide explosives to another student
- Carry any type of drugs or medication, whether illegal, legal, prescribed by a doctor, provided by a parent, or available in stores
- Provide drugs or medication to another student
- Consume alcohol on school property or at a school event
- Provide alcohol to another student
- Smoke cigarettes or use any other tobacco product at school or a school event

- Provide tobacco products to another student
- Commit any sexual act on school premises or at a school event, sometimes including simply hugging or touching another student
- Make a verbal or written threat of violence against other students, teachers, or school staff, even if the threat is made outside of school (such as on a Web site, in an Internet chat room, in a text message, or in a private journal or diary)
- Physically attack or injure another student, teacher, or other school employee
- Destroy school property, including graffiti

Facts About Zero Tolerance Policies in Schools

According to the American Civil Liberties Union, each year more than 1.5 million students miss at least one day of school due to being suspended. According to a survey conducted by the National Center for Education Statistics on student discipline policies for school year 2005–2006:

- Approximately 95% of schools have zero tolerance policies.
- 95% of students ages 12–18 years reported that their school had a student code of conduct.
- 86% of public schools reported at least one crime occurred at their school during the school year.
- 48% of public schools reported taking at least one serious disciplinary action against a student, including expulsion, suspension, and transfer to alternative schools.
- 74% of serious disciplinary actions were suspensions lasting five days or more.
- 5% of serious disciplinary actions were expulsions.
- 20% of serious disciplinary actions were transfers to alternative schools.
- 32% of schools took serious disciplinary action in response to a physical attack or fight.
- 13% of public high schools required student athletes to submit to drug tests.
- 3% of all public schools required students involved in non-athletic extracurricular activities to submit to drug tests.

What You Should Do About Zero Tolerance Policies in Schools

Be Aware of Your School's Policies

Familiarize yourself with your school's rules so that you know what is allowed and what is not. Most schools will make sure that students are well aware of disciplinary policies and student code of conduct. Ask to see a copy of your school's zero tolerance policy and student code of conduct if one is not provided to you. If you have difficulty understanding the rules, discuss them with a parent, teacher, or other adult. Bring up any questions you may have so that you are sure that you understand the policies completely.

Know Your Responsibilities

As long as you are enrolled in a particular school, it is generally a good idea to follow that school's rules to the best of your ability. Make sure you understand how your school's disciplinary policies and student code of conduct apply to you, and decide what you will do if you happen to become involved in a serious situation. For example, will you be held equally responsible for something other students do when you are with them? In this case, will all of you be punished? Are you obligated to report serious misbehavior by another student, such as bringing a gun or other weapon to school? Should you let a teacher or other school employee know if you have heard another student making threats of violence? Thinking about what you would do in these situations beforehand will help you know what to do if anything serious does happen.

Know Your Rights

Student advocacy organizations such as the American Civil Liberties Union, the Parent Advisory Council Team, and Texas Zero Tolerance offer suggestions for what to do if you are involved in a zero tolerance policy violation. These suggestions are intended not as a substitute for the legal advice of an attorney, but rather as general guidelines for you to think about. If you are questioned about a zero tolerance policy violation:

- Be polite and respectful at all times.
- Call your parents or guardian as soon as possible, or ask the school to call them.
- You can insist that your parents or guardian be present while you answer questions.
- You have the right to know the specific things you did that were wrong.
- Do not admit to anything that you did not do or try to cover up for someone else.
- Do not discuss your case with friends or classmates.
- Do not sign any papers without your parents or guardian there to advise you.

Exploring Alternatives

Sometimes zero tolerance policies are controversial because of the way they are written or how they are implemented. The American Civil Liberties Union recommends that school disciplinary policies follow these guidelines:

- Clearly state what is allowed and what is not.
- Clearly state the punishment for rule violations.
- Punishments should not be overly harsh, or more serious than the violation warrants.
- Rules should be easy for the average student to understand.
- Rules should support an improved educational environment.
- Rules should not restrict constitutionally protected activities.
- A copy of the policy should be available to all students.

If you believe your school's zero tolerance policy is unfair, implemented inconsistently, or discriminates against some students, you may be able to influence your school to change the rules. You can start a community group to bring together students and concerned adults to work for a better disciplinary policy. Ask an adult to work with you, or contact local organizations that focus on civil rights or the rights of students for help getting started.

The editors have compiled the following list of organizations concerned with the issues debated in this book. The descriptions are derived from materials provided by the organizations. All have publications or information available for interested readers. The list was compiled on the date of publication of the present volume; the information provided here may change. Be aware that many organizations take several weeks or longer to respond to inquiries, so allow as much time as possible.

Advancement Project
1730 M St. NW, Ste. 910, Washington, DC 20036
(202) 728-9557 • e-mail: ap@advancementproject.org
Web site: www.advancementproject.org

Advancement Project is a legal action group that is committed to racial justice in education. Founded to develop and inspire community-based reform programs, Advancement Project provides support to those working to raise awareness of social inequality and to assist those harmed by racially biased policies in education and throughout society. Its Web site includes a resource center and online library of related publications.

American Civil Liberties Union (ACLU)
132 W. 43rd St., New York, NY 10036
(212) 944-9800 • Web site: www.aclu.org

The ACLU champions the rights set forth in the Declaration of Independence and the U.S. Constitution. It opposes the suppression of individual rights. Its Web site includes a special section for youth, featuring news, issues, and podcasts; a students' rights section provides information about zero tolerance policies in schools.

Children Left Behind Project
c/o Center for Evaluation and Education Policy
509 E. Third St., Bloomington, IN 47401
Web site: ceep.indiana.edu/ChildrenLeftBehind

The Children Left Behind Project focuses on the use and effect of school discipline policies, such as zero tolerance, that rely on school suspension and expulsion as the primary disciplinary measures. The project encourages the exploration and creation of alternatives to student suspension and expulsion.

Children's Defense Fund
25 E St. NW, Washington, DC 20001
(202) 628-8787 • toll-free (800) 233-1200
e-mail: cdinfo@childrensdefense.org
Web site: www.childrensdefense.org

The fund is a nonprofit group founded in 1973 by its president, Marian Wright Edelman, a prominent children's advocate. The fund identifies itself as "the voice for all the children of America" working to "ensure every child a healthy start, a head start, a fair start, a safe start, and a moral start in life and successful passage to adulthood." Its Web site includes an online library of publications on the issues and challenges facing American children today, including education and discipline.

Common Good
1730 Rhode Island Ave. NW, Ste. 308, Washington, DC 20036
(202) 293-7450 • Web site: commongood.org

Common Good is a nonprofit legal reform coalition that is dedicated to "restoring common sense to America." Common Good asserts that American public schools are restricted by too many regulatory policies such as zero tolerance. Its Web site includes an education reform section that provides information designed to help reduce the burden of restrictive school policies.

Educators for Social Responsibility
23 Garden St., Cambridge, MA 02138
(617) 492-1764 • toll-free (800) 370-2515
e-mail: educators@esrnational.org • Web site: www.esrnational.org

Educators for Social Responsibility is a nonprofit organization that works with teachers and school administrators to design and implement policies for the creation of safe, fair schools. Its Web site includes resources and information about school programs such as peer mediation and alternatives to zero tolerance discipline policies.

End Zero Tolerance
c/o Juvenile Law Center
1315 Walnut St., 4th Fl., Philadelphia, PA 19107
(215) 625-0551 • fax: (215) 525-2808
Web site: www.jlc.org/EZT

End Zero Tolerance is an initiative of the Juvenile Law Center, a public interest law firm for children in Pennsylvania and a national advocate for children's legal rights. End Zero Tolerance is dedicated to the elimination of school zero tolerance policies that arrest students. Its Web site provides information on zero tolerance policies as well as resources for individuals and community groups working to end the policies.

Justice Learning
c/o Justice Talking
Annenberg Public Policy Center
3535 Market St., Ste. 200, Philadelphia, PA 19104
(215) 898-9400 • e-mail: jl_info@justicelearning.org
Web site: www.justicelearning.org

Justice Learning is a collaborative educational project of National Public Radio's "Justice Talking" program and the *New York Times* Learning Network. Its Web site provides materials for students interested in the issues and conflicting opinions currently being debated in American society. The Web site includes articles, editorials, and debates on a range of issues related to school policies, including zero tolerance.

Libertarian Rock
e-mail: rockstar@libertarianrock.com • Web site: libertarianrock.com

Libertarian Rock is a Web-based political action group that encourages and assists individuals and organizations who work peacefully and legally to reform what they consider unjust and overly restrictive policies, such as zero tolerance, that affect children and teens. The site provides information, news, and resources for local activists.

National Center for Juvenile Justice
3700 S. Water St., Ste. 200, Pittsburgh, PA 15203
(412) 227-6950
Web site: ncjj.servehttp.com/NCJJWebsite/main.htm

The center is a nonprofit organization that collects and analyzes information on topics related to any aspect of the U.S. juvenile justice system. Its Web site includes a library of research publications and statistical reports, including information on the results of zero tolerance school discipline policies that often channel students into the juvenile justice system.

National Education Association (NEA)
1201 16th St. NW, Washington, DC 20036
(202) 833-4000 • Web site: www.nea.org

The NEA is a volunteer-based organization of educators and academic professionals that works to advance the cause of public education in America so that every child can receive the highest quality education. Its Web site includes information about current issues in school policy development and implementation, including zero tolerance discipline. Online resources are also provided for individuals and communities interested in the quality and safety of their local schools.

National School Safety Center

141 Duesenberg Dr., Ste. 11, Westlake Village, CA 91362
(805) 373-9977 • Web site: www.schoolsafety.us

The center, established by a directive from former U.S. president Ronald Reagan, identifies itself as "an advocate for safe, secure, and peaceful schools worldwide and as a catalyst for the prevention of school crime and violence." Its Web site covers issues related to school safety, emergency readiness, and crisis prevention. An online resource center includes downloadable fact sheets and handouts on specific school safety and discipline issues, including the alternative schools that students expelled under public school zero tolerance policies turn to.

Parent Advisory Council Team (PACT)

e-mail: parentsos@verizon.net • Web site: totallyunjust.tripod.com

PACT is a grass-roots volunteer organization founded by a group of parents who have experienced the negative effects of school zero tolerance policies on their children and families. The group's Web site provides information to educate students and parents about zero tolerance policies and the long-term social, emotional, and educational effects that such policies can have.

SaferSanerSchools

PO Box 229, Bethlehem, PA 18016
(610) 807-9221 • e-mail: usa@safersanerschools.org
Web site: www.safersanerschools.org

SaferSanerSchools is a project of the International Institute for Restorative Practices, a graduate and professional development school in Bethlehem, PA. Working to help educators improve school safety and classroom management, SaferSanerSchools promotes approaches to school discipline that incorporate restorative practices such as conferencing and peer mediation. Its Web site provides links to an extensive collection of online resources and groups that support alternatives to zero tolerance policies as the primary means of student discipline and behavior management.

Texas Zero Tolerance

e-mail: infozt@yahoo.com • Web site: www.texaszerotolerance.com

Texas Zero Tolerance was the first grass-roots, volunteer organization to work against zero tolerance policies in schools and to successfully reform school zero tolerance policies statewide. Its Web site provides information about current school discipline cases, pending legislation related to school discipline policies, and related media reports. An online resource center assists those interested in forming similar organizations in their own state or community, along with information for students affected by school zero tolerance policies.

What Kids Can Do

PO Box 603252, Providence, RI 02906
(401) 247-7665 • e-mail: info@whatkidscando.org
Web site: www.whatkidscando.org

What Kids Can Do is a national nonprofit organization that promotes positive images of young people while emphasizing the potential of young people who are given proper guidance, support, and opportunities for achievement. Its Web site includes an online library of publications and viewpoints written by young people on a range of issues related to education, school discipline, and school policy reform.

BIBLIOGRAPHY

Books

Kern Alexander and M. David Alexander, *The Law of Schools, Students and Teachers in a Nutshell*. St. Paul: West, 2003.

Lorraine Stutzman Amstutz and Judy H. Mullet, *The Little Book of Restorative Discipline for Schools: Teaching Responsibility, Creating Caring Climates*. Intercourse, PA: Good, 2005.

Richard Arum et al., *Judging School Discipline: The Crisis of Moral Authority*. Cambridge, MA: Harvard University Press, 2005.

Mark Boynton and Christine Boynton, *The Educator's Guide to Assessing and Improving School Discipline Programs*. Alexandria, VA: Association for Supervision and Curriculum Development, 2007.

John Devine and Jonathan Cohen, *Making Your School Safe: Strategies to Protect Children and Promote Learning*. New York: Teachers College, 2007.

Alfie Kohn, *Beyond Discipline: From Compliance to Community*. Alexandria, VA: Association for Supervision and Curriculum Development, 2006.

William Lyons and Julie Drew, *Punishing Schools: Fear and Citizenship in American Public Education*. Ann Arbor: University of Michigan Press, 2006.

Mary Ann Manos, *Knowing Where to Draw the Line: Ethical and Legal Standards for Best Classroom Practice*. Westport, CT: Praeger, 2006.

Erica R. Meiners, *Right to Be Hostile: Schools, Prisons, and the Making of Public Enemies*. New York: Routledge, 2007.

Augustina Reyes, *Discipline, Achievement, and Race: Is Zero Tolerance the Answer?* Lanham, MD: Rowman & Littlefield Education, 2006.

Kenneth Saltman and David A. Gabbard, eds., *Education as Enforcement: The Militarization and Corporatization of Schools*. New York: Routledge, 2003.

Randall S. Sprick, *Discipline in the Secondary Classroom: A Positive Approach to Behavior Management*. San Francisco: Jossey-Bass, 2006.

Traci Truly, *Teen Rights (and Responsibilities): A Legal Guide for Teens and the Adults in Their Lives*. Naperville, IL: Sphinx, 2005.

Periodicals

Richard Arum, "For Their Own Good: Limit Students' Rights," *Washington Post*, December 29, 2003.

Kris Axtman, "Why Tolerance Is Fading for Zero Tolerance in Schools," *Christian Science Monitor*, March 31, 2005.

Tom Carroll, "Education Beats Incarceration," *Education Week*, March 26, 2008.

Rick Casey, "Bills Seek to Decriminalize Childhood," *Houston Chronicle*, February 2, 2007.

Michael Crowley, "Kick 'Em Out of School: That's the Cry of the Zero Tolerance Zealots," *Reader's Digest*, May 2004.

Marin Decker, "Curbing School Violence: Researchers Say That 'Zero Tolerance' Policies Are Ineffective," *Deseret Morning News*, January 10, 2005.

Marilyn Elias, "At Schools, Less Tolerance for 'Zero Tolerance,'" *USA Today*, August 9, 2006.

Trent England and Steve Muscatello, "Common Sense on School Violence," *San Diego Union-Tribune*, April 21, 2005.

Helen Eriksen, "Parents Weigh In on Zero Tolerance," *Houston Chronicle*, January 25, 2005.

Jesse Froehling, "Should There Be Zero Tolerance?" *Nogales International*, July 24, 2007.

Catherine Gewertz, "Groups Accuse Florida Districts of Harsh Discipline Approaches," *Education Week*, May 3, 2006.

Dom Giordano, "Why 'Zero Tolerance' Policy Deserves a Zero," *Bulletin* (Philadelphia, PA), June 29, 2007.

Malcolm Gladwell, "No Mercy," *New Yorker*, September 4, 2006.

Maria Glod, "Virginia School's No-Contact Rule Is a Touchy Subject," *Washington Post*, June 18, 2007.

Morgan Josey Glover, "'Good School Climate.' What's It Like?" *News & Record* (Greensboro, NC), July 13, 2007.

Susan Goldsmith, "Unruly Schoolboys or Sex Offenders?" *Oregonian*, July 22, 2007.

Angie Green and Joel Rubin, "L.A. Board of Education Adopts Discipline Policy Aimed at Reducing Suspensions," *Los Angeles Times*, February 28, 2007.

Ray Henry, "Three R's in Today's Schools: Rules, Rules, Rules," *Arizona Star*, June 16, 2007.

Bob Herbert, "6-Year-Olds Under Arrest," *New York Times*, April 9, 2007.

Mary Anne Hess, "The Untolerated: What Happens to Students Who Run Afoul of Strict Discipline Rules?" *NEA Today*, April 2003.

Philip K. Howard, "Class War," *Wall Street Journal*, May 24, 2005.

Trisha Howard and Peter Shinkle, "Keeping Suspended Students in School," *St. Louis Post-Dispatch*, May 24, 2005.

Intelligencer (Wheeling, WV), "Keeping Order in the Classroom," January 19, 2008.

Linda Jacobson, "Guidance Given on Young and Disruptive," *Education Week*, January 16, 2008.

Liz F. Kay, "Code of Conduct Not Fully Enforced, Study Finds," *Baltimore Sun*, April 3, 2005.

Connie Langland, "Controversy over 'Zero Tolerance,'" *Phildelphia Enquirer*, January 23, 2005.

Tamar Lewin, "Research Finds a High Rate of Expulsions in Preschool," *New York Times*, May 17, 2005.

Dave Murray, "BBs to Bombs: Schools Balance Zero-Tolerance Weapons Laws with Details of Case," *Grand Rapids* (MI) *Press*, April 28, 2004.

Rob Nelson, "School Discipline Policies Revisited," *New Orleans Times-Picayune*, October 20, 2006.

Will Okun, "Policing the Halls," *New York Times*, December 6, 2007.

Eddy Ramirez, "School Board Weighs Zero-Tolerance Options: Officials Question Whether One Program Really Discourages

Students' Drug and Alcohol Use," *St. Petersburg* (FL) *Times*, January 25, 2007.

Diane Ravitch, "A Call to Action," *New York Daily News*, February 13, 2005.

Sara Rimer, "Unruly Students Facing Arrest, Not Detention," *New York Times*, January 4, 2004.

Christopher G. Robbins, "Zero Tolerance and the Politics of Racial Injustice," *Journal of Negro Education*, Winter 2005.

Peter Simon, "The Breakdown of Discipline," *Buffalo* (NY) *News*, May 18, 2005.

Kristina Torres, "Schools with Zero Tolerance Stir Critics," *Atlanta-Journal Constitution*, October 27, 2003.

Internet Sources

Alcohol Problems and Solutions, "Zero Tolerance," n.d. www2. potsdam.edu/hansondj/ZeroTolerance.html.

Associated Press, "Has 'Zero Tolerance' in Schools Gone Too Far? Some States' Lawmakers Move in That Direction on Violence, Drugs Policies," MSNBC.com, June 15, 2007. www.msnbc.msn. com/id/19249868.

Radley Balko, "Zero Tolerance Makes Zero Sense," Alcohol Problems and Solutions, n.d. www2.potsdam.edu/hansondj/ YouthIssues/1125513352.html.

Marian Wright Edelman, "The Cradle to Prison Pipeline," Children's Defense Fund, April 27, 2007. www.childrensdefense. org/site/DocServer/NBV_cdf_CPP-report.pdf?docID=4104.

Robin F. Goodman, "Zero Tolerance Policies: Are They Too Tough or Not Tough Enough?" AboutOurKids.org, n.d. www. aboutourkids.org/articles/zero_tolerance_policies_are_they_too_ tough_or-not_tough_enough.

Doug Graves and Laura Mirsky, "American Psychological Association Report Challenges School Zero Tolerance Policies and Recommends Restorative Justice," SaferSanerSchools.org, n.d. www.safersanerschools.org/library/apareport.html.

TheIndyChannel.com, "Have Zero Tolerance Policies Gone Too Far? Some School Districts Reconsidering Policies," March 3,

2004. www.theindychannel.com/education/2893125/detail.html.

JusticeLearning.org, "Zero Tolerance Interactive Timeline," n.d. www.justicelearning.org/justice_timeline/Issues.aspx?issueID=11.

Kevin R. Kosar, "Culture, Discipline, and Schooling," Ednews.org, July 9, 2006. www.ednews.org/articles/1608/1/Culture-Discipline-and-Schooling/Page1.html.

Jonathan McIntire, "No Child Left Behind and Zero Tolerance—An Incongruity!" Council for Exceptional Children, n.d. www.cec.sped.org/AM/Template.cfm?Section=Home&TEMPLATE=/CM/ContentDisplay.cfm&CONTENTID=1252.

Elora Mukherjee, "Criminalizing the Classroom: The Over-Policing of New York City Schools," ACLU.com, March 18, 2007. www.aclu.org/racialjustice/edu/29052pub20070318.html.

NAACP Legal Defense and Educational Fund, "Arresting Development: Addressing the School Discipline Crisis in Florida," Spring 2006. www.naacpldf.org/content/pdf/pipeline/arresting_development_full_report.pdf.

National School Safety and Security Services, "Zero Tolerance: School Safety and Discipline Policies," n.d. www.schoolsecurity.org/trends/zero_tolerance.html.

Phyllis Schlafly, "Zero Tolerance or Zero Common Sense?" EagleForum.org, April 23, 2003. www.eagleforum.org/column/2003/apr03/03-04-23.shtml.

Sharon Smith, "Zero Tolerance Means Jail for Minority Youth," SocialistWorker.org, April 20, 2007. www.socialistworker.org/2007-1/628/628_03_YouthJail.shtml.

John Stein, "To Punish or Not to Punish, That Is the Question," International Child and Youth Care Network, June 2005. www.cyc-net.org/cyc-online/cycol-0605-stein.html.

J.D. Tuccille, "Zero Tolerance under the Microscope," Disloyal Opposition, July 26, 2007. www.tuccille.com/blog/2007/07/zero-tolerance-under-microscope.html.

PICTURE CREDITS